Also by Tom Cooper:
A@W Great Lakes Holocaust: The First Congo War, 1966–1997
A@W Great Lakes Conflagration: The Second Congo War, 1998–2003
A@W Wings over Ogaden: the Ethiopian–Somali War, 1978–1979
A@W Libyan Air Wars: Part 1: 1973–1985
A@W Libyan Air Wars Part 2: 1985–1986
ME@W Syrian Conflagration, 2011–2013

Published by
Helion & Company Limited
26 Willow Road, Solihull, West Midlands,
B91 1UE, England
Tel. 0121 705 3393
Fax 0121 711 4075
Email: info@helion.co.uk
Website: www.helion.co.uk
Twitter: @helionbooks
Visit our blog http://blog.helion.co.uk/

Designed and typeset by Kerrin Cocks,
SA Publishing Services
kerrincocks@gmail.com
Cover design by Paul Hewitt,
Battlefield Design
www.battlefield-design.co.uk
Printed by Henry Ling Ltd, Dorchester,
Dorset

Cover: After completing the rather easy task of conquering Kampala, Tanzanian troops continued their slow advance into northern Uganda. The machine-guner of this Type-62 light tank cheerfully played accordion during the march on Gulu, in late April 1979. (Albert Grandolini Collection)

ISBN 978-1-910294-55-0

British Library Cataloguing-in-Publication Data.
A catalogue record for this book is available from the British Library.

For details of other military history titles published by Helion & Company Limited contact the above address, or visit our website: http://www.helion.co.uk.
We always welcome receiving book proposals from prospective authors.

CONTENTS

GLOSSARY

AB	air base
AB.	Agusta-Bell (Italian helicopter manufacturer)
APC	armoured personnel carrier
ASCC	Air Standardisation Co-ordinating Committee (US, UK, Australian and New Zealand committee for standardisation of designations for foreign [primarily Soviet] armament; its standardisation codenames are usually known as 'NATO designations')
AK	Avtomat Kalashnikova (Kalashnikov assault rifle)
ATGM	anti-tank guided missile
Brig Gen	brigadier general (military commissioned officer rank)
CAP	combat air patrol
Captain	captain (military commissioned officer rank)
C-in-C	commander in chief
CO	commanding officer
COIN	counter-insurgent or counter-insurgency
Colonel	colonel (military commissioned officer rank)
CoS	Chief of Staff
DHC	de Havilland Canada (Canadian aircraft manufacturer)
DMZ	De-militarised Zone
DP	Democratic Party (of Uganda)
DRC	Democratic Republic of the Congo (Congo-Kinshasa)
FRELIMO	*Frente de Libertação de Moçambique* (Liberation Front of Mozambique, armed opposition to Portuguese rule in Mozambique, in 1960–1975; later the ruling party in Mozambique)
FRONASA	Front of National Salvation (armed opposition in Uganda, 1971–1986)
Gen	general
GSU	General Service Unit
HQ	headquarters
IAP	international airport
IDF	Israeli Defence Force
IDF/AF	Israeli Defence Force/Air Force
JWTZ	*Jeshi la Wananchi la Tanzania* (Tanzania People's Defence Force; sometimes cited as the Tanzania People's Defence Force – TPDF – in Western literature)
KIA	killed in action
Km	kilometre
LAAF	Libyan Arab Air Force
LRA	Lord's Resistance Army (armed opposition group in south-western Sudan and northern Uganda)
Lieutenant	Lieutenant
Lieutenant-Colonel	lieutenant-colonel
Major	major
Major-Gen	major-general
MANPADS	man-portable air defence system(s) – light surface-to-air missiles that can be carried and deployed in combat by a single soldier
MBT	main battle tank
MHC	Member of High Command (colonel in the NRA)
MiG	Mikoyan i Gurevich (the design bureau led by Artem Ivanovich Mikoyan and Mikhail Iosifovich Gurevich, also known as OKB-155 or MMZ 'Zenit')
MRLS	multiple rocket launcher system
NRM	National Resistance Movement (umbrella political organisation ruling Uganda from 1986)
OAU	Organisation of African Unity
POW	prisoner of war
PSU	Public Safety Unit
RCAF	Royal Canadian Air Force
SA-3 Goa	ASCC codename for S-125 Neva, Soviet SAM system
SAM	surface-to-air missile
SRB	State Research Bureau
TANU	Tanganyika African National Union (the only legal political party in mainland Tanzania of the 1960–1980 period)
UA	Ugandan Army
UAAF	Ugandan Army Air Force
UK	United Kingdom
UFF	Uganda Freedom Fighters
UFM	Uganda Freedom Movement
UN	United Nations
UNC	Uganda National Congress
UNLA	Uganda National Liberation Army (armed opposition group in Uganda, 1979-1980)
UNRF	Uganda National Rescue Front
UPC	Uganda People's Congress
UPDA	Uganda People's Democratic Army
UPM	Uganda Patriotic Movement
US$	United States Dollar
USSR	Union of Soviet Socialist Republics (or Soviet Union)
WIA	wounded in action

CHAPTER ONE:
INTRODUCTION

This is the first of two works aiming to provide a history of military conflicts in Uganda and Rwanda that raged in these two countries from the 1960s and well into the 1990s. Parts of the story presented here originally came into being as separate overviews of selected African air forces, assembled during years of often troublesome research. Some of these chapters were published on the former ACIG.org, now ACIG.info website, others in printed media like the two-volume book *African MiGs* (see Bibliography for details). An additional impetus for this project came from the work on books *Great Lakes Holocast* (Africa@War Volume 13) and *Great Lakes Conflagration* (Africa@War Volume 14), when it became obvious how narrowly inter-related were several wars fought in Africa since the early 1990s and that there is a need for closer study of relevant military experiences and relations between specific personalities in Uganda, Rwanda and Zaire/Democratic Republic of the Congo. As usual in the case of works of this kind, our research is based on a wide range of sources, including numerous reputable publications, but also some interviews with participants and eyewitnesses. Sadly, with the exception of some European archives, original documentation remains practically inaccessible. Most of what is available are fragments from official archives released by various participants, and even many of these are sometimes fiercely disputed. Through our research and travels, the authors are uncomfortably familiar with the many bloody wars fought in Africa over the last 50 years. We consider any source to be relevant until it can be proven beyond doubt to be without merit. It is a matter of fact that governments, national and private organisations, private companies and certain individuals face harsh ramifications when their influence and/or participation in such conflicts becomes public. The authors therefore carefully collected all the available information, cross-examined various sources, correcting and updating their findings with the aim of offering the most detailed and dependable insight possible, with the objective of providing a comprehensive set of answers to questions like who, when, where, how and why. We have gone to great lengths in order to 'depoliticise' the manuscript. This meant avoiding the use of terms such as 'regime', 'rebels', 'terror' or 'terrorist'. Clearly, one man's 'freedom fighter' is another's 'terrorist'. The reason is that this book does not aim to judge the politics of certain countries. Having no political axe to grind, the authors instead concentrated on recording and describing the military history of the region, and have thus made all efforts to maintain a non-partisan narrative that remains readable and easy to understand.Similarly, in order to simplify the use of this book, all names, locations and geographic designations are as provided in *The Times World Atlas*, or other traditionally accepted major sources of reference.

Geography of Uganda

Uganda lies at the heart of the Great Lakes region of East Africa, the fertile, often humid region centred on Lake Victoria. It is a country of remarkable physical contrasts on a plateau declining gradually from 1,300m (4,300ft) in the south to 750m (2,460ft) in the north. The southern portion is covered by dense forests. Much of the north is open savannah with sparse trees and shrubs, and some semi-desert. The western part of the country is dominated by the Western Rift of the Great Rift Valley – a series of uplifts of the Earth's crust more than 5,000km (3,000 miles) in length. The area is dominated by high mountains of volcanic origin, with the Ruwenzori Range having seven peaks that are covered with snow year-round. Most Ugandan lakes and rivers form a drainage basin for the Nile River, whose principal source is Lake Victoria in the south-east of the country. Other large lakes include Lake Albert, Lake Edward and Lake Kyoga.

Although most of Uganda has distinct dry and wet seasons (the rainy seasons are March to May and October to November), its climate is moderate throughout the year, with average daily temperatures ranging from 18–28°C in January and 17–25°C in July. The area usually receives sufficient rain to permit crops to grow once, often twice a year. The country is situated in an area of rich biodiversity. Plants range from mvuli trees and elephant grass on the plateau to dry thorn scrubs, acacia trees and euphorbia shrubs in the north-east, while papyrus grows in the swamps that surround most of the lakes. Wildlife can only be described as 'spectacular', as Uganda provides habitats for 992 bird species and

A serene scene with buffalo taking a swim in the Nile River near Murchison Falls. (Public-Relations Office of Uganda, via Mark Lepko)

A view of Kampala in 1906. (Rouger. V. Pbas, via Mark Lepko)

A view of Entebbe with Lake Victoria in the background, in 1910. (Couthino & Sons, via Mark Lepko)

338 mammal species, including not only elephants and gorillas but also antelope, chimpanzees, crocodiles, giraffes, lions, leopards, rhinoceroses, zebras and many other species.

Uganda has small amounts of mineral resources, mainly copper, cobalt, nickel, gold, tin, tungsten, beryllium, iron ore, limestone, phosphates and apatite. Oil was discovered only recently and is still not efficiently exploited. Soil and agriculture are therefore the country's most important resources, primarily used for permanent crops such as coffee and bananas. Traditionally, the Ugandan economy has been based on small, African-owned farms since pre-colonial days. Although nearly 10 percent of the land is protected in parks or reserves, demands for farmland, firewood and charcoal are destroying local forests at an alarming rate.

Road networks connect the major urban centres of southern Uganda with the capital Kampala, but more than 90 percent of the roads are dirt or gravel. Railroads link Uganda with Nairobi and Mombasa in Kenya, but, badly neglected for decades, all are in need of upgrade. There are a number of lake ports, including Port Bell (serving Kampala) and Jinja, but steamer traffic on Lake Victoria has been curtailed by the spread of hyacinth weed, which blocks harbours and clogs motors. The Nile is partially navigable in Uganda, but boats cannot pass the Bujagali Falls near Lake Victoria nor Kabalega Falls near Lake Albert. The only international airport is in Entebbe, on Lake Victoria. Modern-day Uganda is divided into 45 districts, including the city of Kampala. The country is bordered by South Sudan to the north; Kenya to the east; Rwanda, Tanzania and Lake Victoria to the south and south-east; and the Democratic Republic of the Congo (DRC) to the west.

Population of Uganda

The population of Uganda is primarily concentrated in the south, particularly in the crescent at the edge of Lake Victoria and in the south-west. Migration and intermarriage has resulted in most Ugandans having ancestors from a variety of 34 ethnic groups. Many presently used languages are not mutually intelligible: about two-thirds of the population speak Bantu languages. These include the largest and wealthiest ethnic group, the Ganda, as well as the Nyankole, Kiga and Soga. About one-sixth are people of Western Nilotic origin, primarily in the north, such as the Langi and Acholi, speaking languages from the Bantu group. Another one-sixth speak an Eastern Nilotic language and live in the north-east, including the Iteso and Karimojong. In the extreme north-west are speakers of Sudanic languages, including the Lugbara and Madi. English is the official language, Swahili is more widely spoken and used as a *lingua franca*, but Luganda – the language of the Ganda – is the most frequently used indigenous tongue. The 1991 census counted 16,671,705 people, primarily black Africans, with less than four percent foreign residents – mostly from neighbouring countries.

The area nowadays within Ugandan borders was originally populated by foragers, possibly Khoisan speakers, until about AD 1000, when Bantu-speaking people moved in. The latter settled primarily in the lower half of the area, before moving east, into the savannah zones around the Great Lakes. There they encountered pastoralists who spoke languages from the Nilo-Saharan family and taught them to cultivate crops. The highly-decentralised nature of northern societies precluded the establishment of states in that area. By comparison, the introduction of plantain as a stable crop permitted dense populations in the area north of Lake Victoria. Over the following centuries, an increasingly centralised political system evolved in this area, giving rise to a number of kingdoms, most of which had an economy based on banana cultivation. One of the early powerful states to emerge was Bunyoro, although even this proved structurally weak due to continual civil wars and royal succession disputes. Legends have it that a refugee from one of many internal Bunyoro conflicts, Kimera, became kabaka (king) of the first modern-day kingdom in this area, Bunyoro-Kitara, which developed after pastoralists known as the Tembuzi began establishing cattle-clientship over the region's agriculturists, around AD 1200. The kingdom of Bunyoro-Kitara expanded its borders when pastoral Binto rulers established themselves in control over numerous smaller agricultural polities, including Buganda, Ankole and Toro, in the 16th Century. Buganda in particular began to play a central role in this history of this area. Its governance was based on a stable succession arrangement, allowing the kingdom to expand its borders and become the dominant power in the region. Bagandan rulers traded ivory and slaves for cloth and firearms brought by merchants from Egypt and Zanzibar, and this trade transformed the kingdom into a wealthy and well-armed country by the time the first European explorers – such as John Hanning Speke and Henry Milton Stanley – passed through the region, in the mid-19th Century, while searching for the source of the Nile River. The wealth of Buganda enabled it to establish an infantry force of up to 125,000 troops and then a navy of up to 230 large outrigger canoes, with the help of which it raided along the shore of Lake Victoria.[1]

The explorers' accounts raised the interest of missionary societies in Europe, and these began establishing missions in the region. British authorities followed hard on their heels: when Britain took control of Egypt, in 1882, it decided to conquer Buganda too and for this purpose signed an agreement with Germany, in 1890, the latter ceding control over the area of present-day Uganda in exchange for British concessions elsewhere in East Africa. Eventually, the influence of foreign missionaries and the struggle between Catholic and Protestant missionaries and converts led to the collapse of royal rule in Buganda. When kabaka Mwanga II attempted to outlaw foreign ideologies, he was deposed by armed converts in 1888. This caused a four-year civil war that ended with victory for Muslim forces, which in turn were defeated by an alliance of Christian groups. War and various epidemics, meanwhile, halved the population and further weakened Buganda, enabling the Protestant missionaries – supported by Nubian mercenaries – to put the area under British control: on 18 June 1894, Uganda was declared a British protectorate. European missionary activity in the 19th Century led to widespread conversion to Christianity. About 41 percent of Ugandans are Roman Catholics and 40 percent are Protestants (mostly belonging to the Anglican Church of Uganda). Protestants developed greater political influence over time, largely during British colonial rule, while Moslems (less than five percent of the population) have less social status.

Despite the declaration of a protectorate and the king of Buganda signing a treaty with agents of the British East Africa Company, allowing the latter to protect the kingdom while the kingdom was not to enter into trade agreements with any other nation, it took Britain several years longer to establish complete control over the area. The British and their Buganda ally engaged in a bloody, five-year long conflict with Bunyoro, then with the Acholi and other people of the north. This forced the Ankole kingdom and chiefdoms of Busonga to also sign treaties with London. Thus came into being the general outline of the modern state of Uganda: a single political entity where none had previously existed, and a state including many ethnically diverse and economically stratified societies at odds with each other long before the advent of European colonialism.

Despite continuous tensions between different ethnic groups, the Uganda Protectorate was generally stable and prosperous, ruled by the British through manipulation of indigenous leaders. Indeed, Uganda can be considered one of the prime examples of their policy of indirect rule in Africa: through a strategy of 'divide-and-rule', the British installed Baganda leaders as local administrators and tax collectors throughout the protectorate – and particularly in areas dominated by other ethnic groups. In turn, they would manipulate traditional local leaders by dividing the lands at their own discretion. Indeed, when resentment towards Baganda sparked in the early 20th Century, the British manipulated various ethnic groups – especially the Bunyoros – against each other and were able to suppress even armed rebellions relatively quickly. Nevertheless, these conflicts persisted for decades and eventually transformed into the core reasons for most wars in Uganda since its independence.

Modern Political History

Anti-colonial agitation in Uganda began in the 1950s, when several youth associations became active, along with more overtly nationalist political parties. Nearly all of these were organised along ethnic lines: even the Uganda National Congress (UNC), formed in 1952 as a countrywide political party, attracted primarily Baganda members. While preparing the colony for independence, Britain granted the Protestant Buganda king, Edward Mutesa II (nicknamed 'Freddie'), real political power. This prompted many other political organisations to start jockeying themselves into position to take power upon independence: the UNC split in 1959, with Apollo Milton Obote forming the Uganda People's Congress (UPC). Another major organisation became the Democratic Party (DP), formed by Roman Catholic Baganda who were intent on preventing Kabaka Freddie from dominating post-colonial Uganda. During pre-independence elections in 1961, the kabaka's supporters – who called themselves the 'King's Friends' – called for a boycott. Consequently, most Baganda did not vote and the ethnically and geographically diverse DP won a majority of seats in the first national assembly. Uganda was granted independence on 9 October 1962, as a parliamentary democracy with the Queen of England and, later, the King of Buganda as ceremonial head of state. In subsequent elections, Obote's UPC allied with the Baganda separatist party, Kabaka Yekka, and this alliance triumphed. Obote became prime minister while Kabaka Freddie was made president. Together, they established Uganda as a federal republic of four semi-autonomous regions: Ankole,

Buganda, Bunyoro and Toro. However, when Obote moved to eliminate Buganda's 'special status' and to return the 'lost countries' to the Bunyoro, his relationship with Freddie began to deteriorate. In order to bolster his political power, Obote began expanding the military and using that expansion as a source of patronage. For this endeavour he built a close relationship with his personal protégé, Idi Amin (who called himself 'Dada', for 'Big Daddy'), one of a small number of African officers in the Ugandan military at the time of independence.In 1966, Obote and Amin faced an official investigation into allegations that they had smuggled gold and ivory out of the Democratic Republic of the Congo (in exchange for provision of arms to one of the secessionist groups). Instead of stepping down, Obote quickly moved to eliminate his opposition: in what was effectively a coup d'état, Amin and the military arrested dissident UPC ministers, enabling Obote to declare himself head of state, suspend the constitution and dissolve the Buganda monarchy. When the Baganda protested, Army units attacked the kabaka's palace, resulting in the Battle of Mengo Hill, after which the king barely managed to escape into exile. Remaining reliant on Amin and the military to maintain order, Obote further consolidated his power by expanding the military and security apparatus, and nationalising businesses. He survived two assassination attempts (in 1969 and 1971) but became suspicious of Amin after the mysterious murder of Acap Okoya, the sole rival to Amin among senior military officers, in early 1970. Being completely reliant upon the military to keep him in power, Obote could take no immediate action against Amin. Instead, he began searching for ways to curb the general's power through placing allies in senior military posts and increasing recruitment of ethnic Acholi and Langi to counter Amin's soldiers from the West Nile region. It was thus only in early 1971 that Obote tried to rid himself of the perceived threat. While leaving for a trip abroad, he ordered the arrest Amin and his closest aides. However, the plot was revealed before it could be carried out and prompted Amin to launch a pre-emptive coup.Idi Amin Dada proved a particularly brutal ruler. Supported by members of the Nubian ethnic group within the military (these staffed the Army's sole tank battalion and much of the military police), he directed his forces to begin a purge. His first target were ethnic Acholi and Langi soldiers, about 5,000 of whom were massacred or disappeared by early 1972. Imposing military law, Amin then launched a massive purge that resulted in the murder of between 300,000 and 500,000 Ugandans over the following years. Attracting Libyan support, Amin expelled all Israeli advisers in early 1972. To gain the favour of Saudi Arabia, he embraced his Islamic heritage and deployed soldiers to aid Egypt during the October 1973 Arab–Israeli War. Meanwhile, in August 1972, he expelled the country's Asian population of about 50,000, which controlled most of the commerce, and distributed their businesses and property to corrupt and incompetent managers.

A column of US-made, but Israeli-delivered M4 Shermans of the 5th Mechanised Regiment UA, during a parade in Kampala in the late 1960s. (Albert Grandolini Collection)

An OT-64 APC of Czechoslovak origin, during a parade in Kampala in the late 1960s. (US DoD)

Amin's bold strokes initially made him popular but because he, like many of the officers he was promoting, was illiterate and corrupt, the economy contracted, shortages became widespread, foreign exchange disappeared and inflation increased. Therefore, despite entering into co-operation with the Soviet Union and wastly expanding the military, Amin lost most of his popular support. On the contrary, tens of thousands of Ugandans – foremost among them all of the surviving Obote loyalists – fled the country. Most of them found refuge in Tanzania, where Amin's principal opponent – President Julius Nyerere – granted them permission to train guerrillas. In 1972, a small rebel force entered Uganda from Tanzania in an attempt to cause a popular uprising to overthrow Amin. The uprising did not materialise and the guerrillas were expelled by the Ugandan Army. Despite this success, Amin's rule remained under constant threat. Surviving a number of assassination attempts, he became increasingly eccentric and paranoid: he constantly purged senior ranks of the military while ordering his security apparatus to intensify the search for any suspected subversives. Eventually, not only did his circle of supporters grow smaller, but several units of the Ugandan Army mutinied in 1978.

To distract the nation's attention from his worsening situation, Amin then ordered loyal troops to invade the Kagera region of Tanzania, initiating the so-called Kagera- or Ugandan-Tanzanian War (also known as the Liberation War in Uganda). Uganda's southern neighbour reacted by mobilising a large army that, together with contingents of Ugandan guerrillas, quickly drove the invaders out of Tanzania. These forces then invaded Uganda and ousted the Amin government, forcing the dictator to flee to Libya in 1979. Although the Kagera War lasted less than eight months, widespread looting by Ugandans and Tanzanians during that period caused as much damage to Uganda's economy as Amin's policies had over the preceding eight years. At least as bad was the subsequent power-struggle in Kampala, which resulted in a particularly bloody civil war, the so-called Ugandan Bush-War. As a result, the economy of Uganda de-facto collapsed, declining about 33 percent by 1986, when the current president, Yoweri Museveni, overthrew Obote's second government. Reforms introduced since 1986 have resulted in a rebound, but it took until the early 2000s for the country to recover the production levels achieved before Amin seized power. Museveni established a mixed presidential and parliamentary system. He appointed an executive cabinet and transformed the military council – which helped him come to power – into a legislative body that had greatly expanded by elections in 1989. Modern-day Uganda is ruled by the National Resistance Movement (NRM), an umbrella political organisation to which all Ugandans nominally belong. Since 1995, the NRM is subject to regulation by parliament and to holding a national conference to elect its chair and other officers. Its political commissar runs the secretariat, which is in charge of political guidance and the military. Activity of other political parties is prohibited, nevertheless, and all candidates compete on a non-party basis (indeed, in a national referendum in 2000, Ugandan voters overwhelmingly chose to retain this non-party system of government rather than switch to a multi-party system).

A Jeep mounting a recoilless rifle (right, foreground) and two Ferret scout cars of British origin, leading a column of Czechoslovak-built OT-64 APCs, sometime in the late 1960s. (US DoD)

A Ugandan pilot disembarking from the cockpit of a Fouga CM.170 Magister training jet. Trained by Israeli instructors who worked in Uganda within the frame of 'Operation Nail' (two of whom can be seen in the background to the left), the UAAF quickly created a small but skilled corps of pilots and ground personnel during the second half of the 1960s. (Tom Cooper Collection)

Military Build-up

The original cadre of the Ugandan armed forces was formed from the former King's African Rifles, an element of the British colonial army in East Africa, and most officers were British. Britain provided most of the early training and equipment, and many Ugandans were trained in the UK during the 1960s.[2] At independence, there was only one force, the 1st Battalion Uganda Rifles, of 700 troops. The manpower requirements were easily met by voluntary enlistment and by July 1963 the number of trained troops was increased to 1,500. Because it was deemed necessary to face both internal and external threats (including potential threats from the DRC and Sudan), plans were drawn up to form the 2nd

Magisters during a training flight in the late 1960s. All aircraft were left in the colours already applied in Israel – including brown (the RAL 8008) and blue (the RAL 5008) on the top and side surfaces, and light grey (the RAL 7044) on the under-surfaces. Visible are serials (clockwise): U100 (top left corner), U101 (formation leader), U100 (top left corner), U105 and U106. (Albert Grandolini Collection)

One of six C-47 Dakota transports acquired from Israel and operated by the UAAF in the late 1960s. They were camouflaged in the same colours as the Israeli-delivered Magisters. (Albert Grandolini Collection)

The UAAF acquired two Piper PA-23-250 Aztecs in 1968 and used them for liaison and reconnaissance. They wore serials U-301 and U-302. (Albert Grandolini Collection)

A rare photograph of one of the L-29s purchased from Czechoslovakia in 1967. All the Delfins were originally camouflaged in colours similar but slightly darker than those used on the Israeli-delivered Magisters, and wore serials in the range between U-101 and U-114, applied in black (these were repeated on the top of the right and underside of the left wing). (Albert Grandolini Collection)

Battalion, which came into being in January 1964, primarily with help from Israeli advisers.[3]

On 20 January, there was an Army mutiny in neighbouring Tanganyika and Kenya. This was duplicated in Uganda on 23 January 1964, when the 1st Battalion mutinied because of soldiers' discontent about their condition of services. Although the uprising was quelled with British assistance, the Army was eventually successful in gaining its demands. Obote's government offered a number of major concessions, foremost in regards of a near-immediate Africanisation of the officer corps and significant increase of military wages. Major Idi Amin Dada was appointed the CO of the 1st Battalion. Nevertheless, the government went as far in April 1964 as to create the (Israeli-trained) General Service Unit (GSU) of the police – a unit of about 800 trained in riot control – as its own security guard stationed around Kampala.

While ordering the withdrawal of the British Army contingent, in July of the same year, Kampala intensified co-operation with Israel, launching efforts to create an air force along with armour, artillery and paratroop units.[4] Related efforts were further intensified by the Congo crisis and an attack of Congolese combat aircraft on two border villages in the West Nile District, on 13 February 1965. Two weeks after this attack, the 3rd Battalion was officially established at Mubende, and the 4th Battalion came into being by the end of March 1965. With six additional units created by 1 July 1965, the Ugandan Army (UA) – officially declared as such on 1 August 1965 – was able to establish its 1st Brigade. At that time, the UA totalled about 4,500 officers and other ranks (the majority were northerners), including those assigned to the Brigade Signals Squadron, Brigade Reconnaissance Squadron and support services such as the Army Ordnance Depot, UA Workshops, Brigade Signals Squadron Training Wing, Records Office and the Pay and Pension Office. After Obote's coup and abrogation of the constitution in 1966, the UA was lavished with an ever-increasing budget: this totalled 10 percent more than that of Kenya and Tanzania combined.[5] By 1969, heavy equipment included 12 M4A1(76)W Sherman tanks, up to 20 Ferret armoured cars and 12 Czechoslovak-built OT-64B APCs.[6]

The Military Police of the UA was officially established on 1 January 1967 (the majority of its troops recruited in the West Nile District), and by 1970, the military included the 1st Brigade (HQ in Mbale), 2nd Brigade (Nakasero), Paratroop Battalion, a Border Guard Unit (Gul) and the 5th ('Malire') Mechanised Regiment. By that time, up to 61 percent of military personnel were northerners; only 22 percent were Easterners and 12 percent Westerners. While the entire armed forces (including the GSU) totalled about 9,800 personnel, the officer corps still numbered only 200 in August 1968.[7]

Ugandan Army Air Force

Israeli military assistance was also instrumental in the establishment of the Ugandan Army Air Force (UAAF) in 1964. The first three Ugandan pilots were trained in Israel, and Israel sold the UAAF its first combat aircraft, including nine Fouga CM.170 Magisters jet trainers and light strikers and six Douglas

C-47 transports. Thanks to co-operation with Czechoslovakia and the USSR, and with continuous Israeli assistance, a small but well-balanced and -trained air force came into being during the mid-1960s, with most of its pilots and ground personnel being of native origin.[8]

In July 1965, Kampala and Moscow signed a contract that granted the supply of five Mikoyan i Gurevich MiG-17Fs and two MiG-15UTIs, military maintenance facilities, spare parts, communication equipment and weapons to the UAAF. Also included was the training of 250 Ugandan personnel – including 20 pilots and 50 technicians – in the USSR. In support of this project, the Soviet Union deployed at least 25 Soviet instructors to Uganda. These arrived in 1966, together with the first MiGs, and apparently worked at least parallel to Israeli instructors. A number of additional MiG-17s were later to be acquired by the UAAF. Meanwhile, Kampala and Prague signed a contract for the acquisition of 14 L-29 Delfins.[9] Their deliveries and initial service in Uganda was supported by a group of Czechoslovak advisers (for a list of these, see Table 1), who arrived in the country in November 1967 – only to find their duty there extremely complicated by a lack of adequate ground support and navigation equipment at Gulu AB.

Table 1: Czechoslovak Advisers in Uganda

Rank & Name	Date of Birth	Place of Birth		Position in Advisery Group
Colonel Jaroslav Hlado	8 May 1913	Novy Jicin	Senior officer at Foreign Training Department; Main Directorate of Air Force and Air Defence Force	commander
Major Otakar Simek	5 November 1930	Rokytnice	Navigator, 4th Aviation Training Regiment	pilot-instructor
Captain Rudolf Sochor	9 September 1936	Hradec Kralove	Pilot-instructor, 4th Aviation Training Regiment	pilot-instructor
Lieutenant-Colonel Josef Blaha	26 June 1924	Pchery	Instructor for theory and design of airframes	operation and maintenance technician
Captain Jan Valdman	3 February 1934	Horne Oresany	Operation inspector, 2nd Aviation Training Regiment	repair technician
Captain Viktor Remenec	23 December 1936	Telgart	Senior instructor for electric equipment	specialist technician for electronic equipment
Major Frantisek Platil	21 November 1933	Praha	Senior instructor for radio equipment	technician for radio equipment
Major Veroslav Brychta	25 March 1935	Vracov	Senior instructor for armament	technician for armament
Lieutenant-Colonel Josef Susa	1 March 1914	Chlum	Chief interpreter and translator	interpreter
Lieutenant-Colonel Bedrich Jurnikl	31 March 1928	Bilovice nad Svitavou	Senior officer at Foreign Training Department, Main Directorate of Air Force and Air Defence Force	interpreter

The first three Delfins were unloaded at the Gulu railway station in late May 1967. They were assembled by Czechoslovak officers in late November, but not without significant problems, as crates with aircraft and their parts were stored outside hangars for nearly five months, at the mercy of the weather and termites. It took the Czechoslovaks some very hard work, plenty of talent and skill in improvisation to assemble and then bring the aircraft into working order – only to find out that the L-29s arrived without any flying helmets and parachutes for pilots. Furthermore, although marketed to the Ugandans as light attack aircraft, no suitable bombs or unguided rockets were delivered. Weapons arrived only in spring 1969, together with a consignment of spare parts, by when the activity of Czechoslovak advisers was extended for another year. The last L-29 ordered by Kampala was only delivered some time later that year, and the Czechoslovaks were then asked to convert to the type a group of Ugandan pilots originally trained in Israel. By 1970, the UAAF thus operated a total of 16 Piper PA-18 Super Cubs and Piper PA-23-250 Aztecs, four Piaggio P-149s, 14 L-29s, nine CM.170 Magisters, five MiG-17Fs, two MiG-15UTIs, one de Havilland Canada DHC-4 Caribou and six C-47 transports from bases in Entebbe and Gulu. Very little is known about the organisational structure of the force. It seems that there were four units, with one of two operational squadrons – both of which were based at Entebbe – flying L-29s and Magisters, and the other MiG-17s. All transports were operated by the third unit, while all the training aircraft were concentrated within one training establishment. In the mid-1960s, an additional air base was constructed by the Israelis near Nakasangola, in northern Uganda.[10]

Training in Czechoslovakia

While no specific details about the training of UA personnel in Israel or the USSR became available, and very little is known about the few Ugandan pilots who underwent advanced courses in the UK in the early 1970s, the availability of documentation from the National Archives of the Czech Republic in Prague enables a better insight into the training of Ugandan pilots and technicians in the former Czechoslovakia. The first military contacts between the two countries were established in March

A still from a video showing two Ugandan L-29 Delfin jet trainers sometime in the early 1970s. By this time the serials of UAAF Delfins were changed to the range between U-501 and U-514. (Albert Grandolini Collection)

The Ugandan Police used to operate a small air wing equipped with at least one DHC-4 Caribou (registration 5X-AAB), acquired in June 1965, and two Westland Scout light helicopters (including one registered as 5X-UUW). Nothing is known of their eventual fate. (Albert Grandolini Collection)

A still from the same video, showing the L-29 with serial number U-504, following an overhaul and complete re-painting with beige and dark green on the top surfaces and sides, and light admiralty grey on the under-surfaces. (Albert Grandolini Collection)

1964, when Major Adoko – acting as Obote's representative in Prague – contacted Czechoslovak foreign minister Vaclav David, enquiring about the possibility for the training of between seven and nine Ugandan soldiers in combined arms reconnaissance. According to Adoko, this requirement was part of an effort to reduce the influence of English-speaking and Israeli military advisers in his country. It seems that related talks resulted in no agreement. Nevertheless, as Czechoslovakia soon after established a representative office in Kampala, a Czechoslovak Charge d'Affairs named Stadler informed Prague about Ugandan interest in the acquisition of 'special equipment' and training of fighter pilots. The Czechoslovak government promptly turned down this request because the Ministry of Foreign Trade mistakenly thought that Ugandans expected the training of their pilots to be free of charge. However, no sooner had the Czechoslovak officials found out that Uganda was willing to pay in hard currency, than they reacted positively and on 17 May 1965 a Czechoslovak business delegation – including Colonel Mikuals Singlovic (from the Ministry of Defence) and Jiri Chlapik (Ministry of Foreign Trade) – arrived in Kampala. During a stay that lasted longer than a month, Singlovic and Chlapik arranged Contract 5252 for the training of 10 Ugandan pilots and 18 maintenance personnel on Aero L-29 Delfin jet trainers for a duration of 29 months in Czechoslovakia. Furthermore, the contract stipulated that the training of pilots was to be run in three phases, including basic (lasting 17 months), advanced and combat, of which the former was to be run in Czechoslovakia and the latter two at Gulu AB in Uganda. Eventually, all the training was run in Europe because the UAAF proved unable to provide adequate facilities. Indeed, instead of the planned 17 months, the basic training phase lasted no less but 27–28 months for pilots and 26–27 months for technicians.[11]

Training of Ugandan pilots in Czechoslovakia began on 2 July 1965 (for the names of pilots and their total number of flights and flying hours, see Table 2). Generally, Ugandan students proved quite talented and pilots not only completed their basic training without problems, but also fully mastered the L-29. Ground personnel could complete the operational service of this aircraft type, including regular maintenance and replacement of engines.[12] Nevertheless, some did experience problems of a different nature. Student technician Joseph Oryema was sent home on 26 December 1966 because of permanent nervous illness, while student pilot Abdunulu Kagalula was dismissed from training for lack of discipline.

Table 2: Ugandan Pilots Trained in Czechoslovakia, 1965–1967

Name	Totals for preliminary, basic, advanced and combat training on Zlin Z-326 Trener Master and L-29 Delfin jet trainers in Czechoslovakia	
	Flights	Flying Hours
David Emadit	524	189.24
Joseph Ageimo Essimu	524	192.22
Eneriko Utulu Tassas	560	197.50
Zeddy Maruru Byatoraki	554	192.02
Dick Keith Sekiwano	527	190.41
Chirstopher Haig Mukwaya	527	190.14
Norman Otunu Lakor	547	195.31
Zachary Alex Oryang	542	195.25
Jackson Okello	558	195.54
Abdunulu Kagula (dismissed because of indiscipline)	362	110.33

Because of an over-dependence on the military for the survival of Obote's government, Major-General Idi Amin began playing an increasingly influential role in Ugandan politics in the late 1960s. (Albert Grandolini Collection)

During the last phase of training, the scope of the course was widened to include more general knowledge to help the involved pilots build up and develop an air force. In the course of this stage, the study interest and morale of the Ugandans improved sharply as they started to clearly realise their responsibility for the future of the Ugandan Army Air Force. Nevertheless, their instructors concluded that not only pilots but technicians too would still need additional training in order to become fully self-sufficient in their duties.Meanwhile, back in Uganda, disagreements developed between Colonel Jaroslav Hlado and some of his Czechoslovak colleagues in January 1970. Officially, the reasons were of a political nature, but unofficially, one of the advisers attempted to conceal an unauthorised engine repair. Although Obote personally intervened, announcing that the training contract would be extended if Hlado would remain in his position, political commissars in Prague decided to remove him: Hlado was withdrawn from Uganda and sent into early retirement in 1971.[13]

CHAPTER TWO:
AN AFRICAN COLD WAR

Political instability in Uganda and brutal prosecution of oppositionals caused many Ugandans to leave their country. Most of them have found refuge in Tanzania, the geopolitical position and policy objectives of which have resulted in it becoming a logical haven for a multitude of guerrilla movements dedicated to overthrowing different governments in neighbouring countries of the 1960s and 1970s. The Tanzanian government at least ignored – if not openly supported – at least a few of the several dozen insurgent movements from abroad within its borders over time: more often it was either not willing or unable to do anything against them, or of providing direct military assistance to most of the groups in question. Nevertheless, a select few did receive bases, training, arms, supplies and shipments of arms – primarily from China. This sometimes exposed the country to retaliation attacks from Rhodesia, reconnaissance flights over its territory by Portuguese aircraft from neighbouring Mozambique and sporadic border incidents. Before long, this situation also placed Tanzania on a collision course with Uganda.

Amin's Coup d'état of 1971

By January 1971, Obote's administration was highly unpopular. It not only became notorious for terror and harassment of the population, but also proved inept and massively corrupt, and was causing frequent food shortages. Against this backdrop, while preparing to travel for the 1971 Commonwealth Heads of Government Meeting in Singapore, Obote ordered loyal Langi officers to arrest Amin and his supporters in the military. Israeli advisers in Kampala learned about this plot and warned Amin, whom they considered a useful agent to de-stabilise Sudan.[14] Meanwhile, promoted in rank to Major General and Commander-in-Chief of the Ugandan Army and Ugandan Army Air Force, Idi Amin ordered his mechanised regiment and military police to strike first. Early on the morning of 25 January 1971, they took over strategic installations around Kampala and Entebbe International Airport (IAP), easily overcoming the rather disorganised opposition of troops loyal to Obote. Almost straight away, Amin ordered mass executions of Acholi and Lango officers and other ranks known as loyal to the former president.Although warmly welcomed by most of the people of the Buganda kingdom (which Obote had attempted to dismantle), and announcing his intention to play a mere 'caretaker role' until the country could recover for civilian rule, Amin subsequently imposed a military dictatorship. Because he was illiterate, he governed with oral orders, issued either personally or via the telephone to his commanders. He renamed the Government House 'the Command Post', instituted an advisery defence council composed of military commanders, appointed loyal soldiers to top government posts and parastatal agencies, placed military tribunals above the system of civil law and informed the few remaining civilian cabinet ministers that they would be subjected to military discipline.While the military was hit by a series of purges and desertions, and left to loot and kill as its commanders wanted, recruitment was intensified: up to 19,742 new troops were taken in during 1971, theoretically increasing the total to about 27,000 officers and other ranks. Actually, a reshuffling of the officer corps and promotions based solely on loyalty to the new strongman resulted in widespread indiscipline: by the end of the year, only around 11,409 men were with their units, while 15,764 were simply 'unaccounted for'. The

Major-General Idi Amin hours after the coup in which he installed himself in power in Kinshasa, on 25 January 1971. Amin's rise to power was initially warmly welcomed by the Ugandan population. (Albert Grandolini Collection)

The driver of this M4 Sherman tank was photographed with his vehicle parked outside Amin's house in Kampala, reading a newspaper, on 25 January 1971. The registration of his vehicle (usually applied in white on a black field) was 05UA85, standing for the 85th vehicle of the 5th Regiment UA. (Albert Grandolini Collection)

primary reason for the near-anarchy that spread through the UA was fierce rivalries between officers – especially those trained in the UK and those in or by the Israelis: these turned the military into an arena of lethal competition, in which losers were usually eliminated.[15]Amin further worsened the situation by not only ordering the narrowing of the recruitment base to Sudanese-speakers, and especially Muslims, but also juggling the top military personnel in order not to let them find time or opportunity to build influence in particular positions. Early on during his rule, a majority of new recruits were Kakwa, Nubians and foreigners. Although most of them were enlisted to serve with the military, many more filled newly-established security agencies. While disbanding the notorious GSU, Amin recruited thousands of new troops from what is nowadays South Sudan for the 3,000-strong State Research Bureau (SRB) and 350-strong Public Safety Unit (PSU), the Military Police, Anti-Corruption Squad (led by Bob Astles) and Special Presidential Intelligence Office – all of which were directly responsible to the new president. In particular, the SRB HQ at Nakasero became the scene of torture and thousands of executions over the following years.[16]Reports of those tragic times by Czechoslovak advisers present in Uganda indicate that most UAAF personnel trained in Czechoslovakia became victims of purges and massacres, as the majority of them were from Acholi and Lango tribes. Nevertheless, Prague continued the delivery of other 'special equipment' ordered by Kampala, foremost among them OT-64 SKOT APCs, even when such activities became a matter of major embarrassment for Czechoslovakia because of the notoriety of Amin's rule. Indeed, although the Ugandan economy was soon on the verge of collapse and Kampala proved unable to pay for all the delivered goods, nine Czechoslovak military advisers – including those responsible for maintenance of L-29s and OT-64s – remained in the country.

Tanzanian Background

Widespread atrocities, random massacres, looting, corruption and prosecution of oppositionals by Amin's administration caused thousands of Ugandans to flee to the United Republic of Tanzania. This country came into being on 26 April 1964, when the states of Tanganyika (a former German colony until 1916, then British-administered until 1961) and Zanzibar (a former British colony, which gained independence in 1963 and was ruled by an Arab Sultan for a year) were united. Nearly five times the size of Uganda, Tanzania has a population almost three times bigger, composed of a plethora of more than 120 different tribes, linguistic and religious groups. The official capital is Dodoma, where the president's office, the National Assembly and some government ministries are located. However, former capital Dar es-Salaam is not only the country's largest city, principal port and leading commercial centre, but also retains most government offices.[17]Although Tanzania has been spared the sort of tribal dissensions that have created severe internal security problems elsewhere in Africa, it has faced a multitude of dangerous ethnic, political and economic divisions between its people. Nevertheless, none of the local tribes are large or powerful enough to constitute an independent political threat to the federal government. Similarly, the Arab, Asian and European populations are too small to threaten each other and the established order. The religious divisions between Christians, Moslems and followers of native religions were more significant, but led to no disorder. All this has served to minimise ethnic differences among the population. Tanzania borders Uganda and Kenya to the north; Mozambique, Malawi and Zambia to the south; and Burundi, Rwanda and the DRC to the west. Despite some border disputes with Malawi, the country traditionally maintains cordial relations with most of its neighbours.

Tanzanian infantry during a parade in June 1965 (staged to celebrate a high-ranking visit from China). (Albert Grandolini Collection)

Tanzania People's Defence Force

The original core of the Tanzanian military was formed around the British-organised and run 1st Battalion Tanganyika Rifles. This unit mutinied over pay, promotions and the removal of British officers in January 1964, and was subsequently disbanded, despite the government's understanding of the reasons for the mutiny. Subsequently, a new military was established consisting of new recruits.

The new Tanzanian military – officially named the *Jeshi la Wananchi la Tanzania* (JWTZ – Tanzania People's Defence Force), in 1965 – was completely remodelled and differed greatly from the defence establishment in other former British nations. Civilian control was exercised directly by the President Nyerere, although nominally all defence matters were under the jurisdiction of the Office of the Second Vice-President.[18] The First Vice-President (who by the terms of the Tanganyika-Zanzibar merger of April 1964 was also the President of Zanzibar) was also the nominal head of the Zanzibar portions of the armed forces. De-facto it was the Chief of Staff – Major-Genaral Mrisho S. H. Sarakikya (from 1964 until 1974) – who actually commanded the entire military establishment.Further down the chain of command, Tanzanian military leaders did not follow any specific foreign model when creating the JWTZ: they *organised* their units – grouped into a total of four reinforced brigades – the way they found suitable for them. Similarly, they went to great lengths to let their future officers receive an education in the most diverse military disciplines: while many were schooled in communist countries, others visited Western military academies. Thus while some officers were taught guerrilla warfare in China, others learned counter-insurgency warfare at Sandhurst in Great Britain.

Tanzania's foreign policy is traditionally non-aligned and neutral, in turn enabling the country to seek and accept development aid and military assistance from all quarters. While the initial provision of arms was British, Canada, China, Indonesia, Israel, the Netherlands, Soviet Union and West Germany provided military advice and equipment through most of the 1960s and 1970s. China was most active in this regards: it trained and equipped the police (Israel has trained a company of about 200 police paratroops); it donated 14 Type-62 light and 16 Type-59 medium battle tanks (MBTs), 15 BTR-152 ACPs, 32 mortars, an undisclosed number of anti-aircraft (AA) cannons and machine guns, and the mass of light arms for the military, and it was China that provided patrol boats for the JWTZ Navy.[19] Contrary to the usual practice of grouping armour and artillery into separate units, Tanzania tended to assign the few tanks, howitzers and mortars into a 'Task Force' assigned to each of four brigades that were established over time. Therefore, JWTZ brigades were quite

A Ugandan soldier manning the ZPU-4 quad 14.5mm calibre anti-aircraft machine gun on the streets of Kampala on 27 January 1971. (Albert Grandolini Collection)

A Chinese variant of the Soviet-designed M1939 37mm calibre automatic anti-aircraft cannon during a military parade in 1965 held at Zanzibar Island, following the unification of Zanzibar with Tanganiyka to form Tanzania. (Albert Grandolini Collection)

powerful formations each totalling about 4,000 officers and other ranks. As a whole, the JWTZ was heavily politicised and more often engaged in development work than in regular military exercises. On the other hand, it was based on a merit-oriented promotion system that was to prove highly effective during the coming years. Due to the large supply of an available workforce, the JWTZ needed no conscription: enlistment was for a two-year term. But the bulk of recruits came from the National Service Corps (NSC). The NSC was developed parallel to the JWTZ – indeed, as a counterweight to the military – and was obligatory for all high-school- and college-graduated males aged 18 to 35.In March 1965, the Tanzanian Parliament launched an effort to create Field Force Units in each region and to give members of the Police Force, Prison Service, the NSC and Youth League of the Tanganyika African National Union (TANU) full military training with modern weapons.[20]

Another view of the same weapon. Generally, all the heavy armament donated by the PRC to the Tanzanian military was camouflaged in olive green. (Albert Grandolini Collection)

A column of Type-62 light tanks of the JWTZ during a parade in 1970. All were painted in olive green and wore large markings on their turrets. Visible are tanks marked as 1B, 2B and 3B. (Albert Grandolini Collection)

A JWTZ truck towing what looks like the M1942 (ZiS-3) 76.2mm calibre divisional gun, either of Soviet origin or donated by China. (Albert Grandolini Collection)

Air Wing

A small transport and liaison air arm, named Usafirashaji wa Anga (Air Wing) was established within the JWTZ Air Defence Command in early 1965, when 10 Tanzanian students were sent to West Germany for pilot training. West Germany intended to provide extensive assistance to the JWTZ, including deliveries of Piaggio P.149D basic trainers, Dornier Do 27 and Do 28 light transports, as well as Noratlas transports. However, within a few weeks all such plans had to be abandoned amid differences between the West German and Tanzanian governments over the presence of an East German ambassador in Dar es-Salaam, as well as West German involvement in deliveries of aircraft to Portugal – then involved in fighting insurgents in neighbouring Mozambique. Correspondingly, only eight disassembled Focke-Wulf-built P.149Ds arrived at Dar es-Salaam, where they remained stored for a lengthy period of time before entering service.Canada, keen to gain a foothold in Tanzania since 1963, took the place of West Germany and in 1965 launched a project worth US$10.5 million with the aim of bolstering the JWTZ. The future air arm would include one or two squadrons of combat aircraft to counter Portuguese and Rhodesian forces. Canada initially provided 80 instructors from the Royal Canadian Air Force (RCAF), these arriving in January 1966 with the intention of establishing the necessary infrastructure. Simultaneously, 24 Tanzanians travelled to Canada to receive training as pilots and ground personnel. A number of de Havilland Canada DHC-3 Otter and DHC-4 Caribou transports were readied to be used by the Tanzanians in Canada, as well as for delivery to the JWTZ. Once in Dar es-Salaam, the Canadians assembled the P.149Ds delivered from West Germany and launched a local training programme for Tanzanians. Thus, by May 1967, the JWTZ operated eight DHC-3s, three DHC-4s and eight P.149Ds, and by the end of the year possessed a small cadre of well-trained pilots and ground personnel. However, co-operation with Canada came to an end in 1968 when the Tanzanian government decided to establish close ties with China instead.

China had established a relationship with Tanzania during 1964 and provided substantial aid grants in the following years. Among other projects, the Chinese completely built, equipped and staffed a police college at Moshi, and over 13,000 Chinese workers helped construct the 2,000-km (1,243-mile) Tanzania–Zambia railroad, from Kapiri Mposhi to Dar es-Salaam. In 1970, a sizeable contingent of Chinese military advisers arrived with the intention of constructing a major air base near Ngerengere, then some 140km

(87 miles) outside Dar es-Salaam, as well as preparing the JWTZ for an introduction to jet fighters. During the same year, 170 Tanzanian military personnel travelled to China to be trained as pilots and ground personnel.Limited connections with Canada remained intact, however, and in 1970 Tanzania ordered eight additional DHC-4s, all of which were delivered the following year, by which time the JWTZ started selling its DHC-3s. Using Canada as an intermediary, the US delivered four Piper PA-28-140 Cherokees in 1971 to reinforce the fleet of tired P.149D basic trainers.

First Blood

The first clash between Uganda and Tanzania occurred only a few months after Amin's coup, on 25 August 1971. According to Ugandan sources, it was caused by Tanzanians hijacking four UA troops. At the time, Abdu Kisuule was in command of a company from the 5th Mechanised Specialist Reconnaissance Regiment (colloquially the 'Malire Regiment'), ordered to launch a rescue operation:

I mobilized six APCs, arranging them in numbers and putting my senior and most experienced APC driver, Sgt Hussein Doka, in the lead APC where I was too. The plan was that when the security guards at the Ugandan side of the border see my APCs coming, they just open the border gate and we go through at full speed to force our way into Tanzania. With all the six APCs ready, I entered the lead one and raised the other five on the radio, ordering them to move out. That was the last order I gave and we moved at full speed towards the border. The security did as we had planned, opening the border entrance long before we reached [it]. We went straight into Tanzania.

I was looking through my binoculars when we entered Tanzania. The last thing I recall was seeing a small red light at a distance. My APC was hit and I was badly wounded. My rib cage was blown open, leaving my lungs hanging [out], with the diaphragm destroyed.Before I lost consciousness, I asked Sgt Doka, 'Are you hit?' He said, 'No.' I told him to turn left or right and take my body back to Uganda. By the time I regained consciousness, the APC had been stuck in mud inside Tanzania. Sgt Doka and the gunner had run away, leaving a few recruits and me in the APC. Fortunately, the recruits were not hurt.

After this unpleasant experience, Amin issued a strict set of Rules of Engagement (ROEs) for any future confrontations with Tanzania, stressing that UA officers could launch attacks into that country only if:

1. Amin gave the order to attack;
2. Tanzanians attacked Uganda; or
3. if any Ugandan soldiers were captured or if Tanzanians started shelling Uganda.

Regardless of the subsequent developments, these ROEs were to hold for the next seven years.[21]

Chaos in Uganda

Throughout 1972 and 1973, Amin began experiencing ever-increasing problems with maintaining control over the anarchy he caused in Uganda. Nevertheless, he continued making controversial and eccentric decisions. Early in 1972, the Ugandan strongman came up with the idea to invade Tanzania with the objective of obtaining a corridor to the Indian Ocean. For this purpose he requested Israel to sell an additional batch of Sherman tanks and lend 24 McDonnell Douglas F-4E Phantom II fighter-bombers to Uganda. When the Israelis refused, Amin closed their embassy and severed diplomatic relations. He later turned the Israeli ambassador's house over to Palestinian groups and sent a message to United Nations (UN) secretary general Kurt Waldheim in which he said that he was able to understand why Adolf Hitler had killed six million Jews.Stating that they had 'frustrated the attempts by Ugandan Africans to participate in the economic and business life of the country', on 9 August 1972 Amin decreed that British Asians and citizens of India, Pakistan, and Bangladesh must get out of Uganda within 90 days or 'face the consequences'. Estimates vary as to how many fled the country to face uncertain futures in Britain or elsewhere, but most reliable accounts cite about 40,000. All small and medium-sized businesses and residences were allocated to Ugandan citizens. The value of the goods in any store previously owned by Asians was treated as a loan by the government, which took over the large Asian-owned businesses, sugar estates, hotels and factories. Also nationalised were about 30 British-owned business and tea estates. Continuing the shift in allegiance from being a pro-Western ruler and seaching for new sources of funding, Amin next established ties with King Faisal of Saudi Arabia, who began providing financial support.[22] In January 1973, Libyan strongman Muammar Muhammad Abu Minyar al-Gaddafi visited Kampala: in exchange for Amin becoming an outspoken critic of Israel, providing training bases for Palestinian militants and deploying a small UA contingent to Egypt, Gaddafi also began providing financial aid. As a sign of appreciation, the Jinja Barracks were subsequently re-named the Gaddafi Garrison Unit.

Obote's Rushed Invasion of 1972

As Ugandan oppositionals began to gather in Tanzania, President Nyerere refused to officially recognise Amin's rule over Uganda. Instead, he granted permission for Obote and his followers to establish a training camp at Kingolwira, about 200km from Dar es-Salaam. Training at that site began in late March 1971, and by August of that year 294 insurgents were ready. However, Obote's original plan to launch a two-pronged invasion from Tanzania and Sudan was called off due to concerns that Israel and Great Britain had learned about his intentions and would support Amin.[23]

Meanwhile, a much smaller group of Ugandan exiles gathered around Yoweri Kaguta Museveni in Dar es-Salaam. Born in 1944 in Rwampara County of south-western Uganda, Museveni came from a family of illiterate cattle-herders. His mother belonged to a powerful Hima clan of the former Ankole Kingdom, which used to have a social structure similar to the Rwandan one. He became attracted by politics and sympathised with the DP during studies at secondary school. He opted to study at the University of Dar es-

Youthful recruits of the NSC during a parade in the late 1960s. (Albert Grandolini Collection)

Idi Amin with several of his top commanders and two sons, in the mid-1970s. (Mark Lepko Collection)

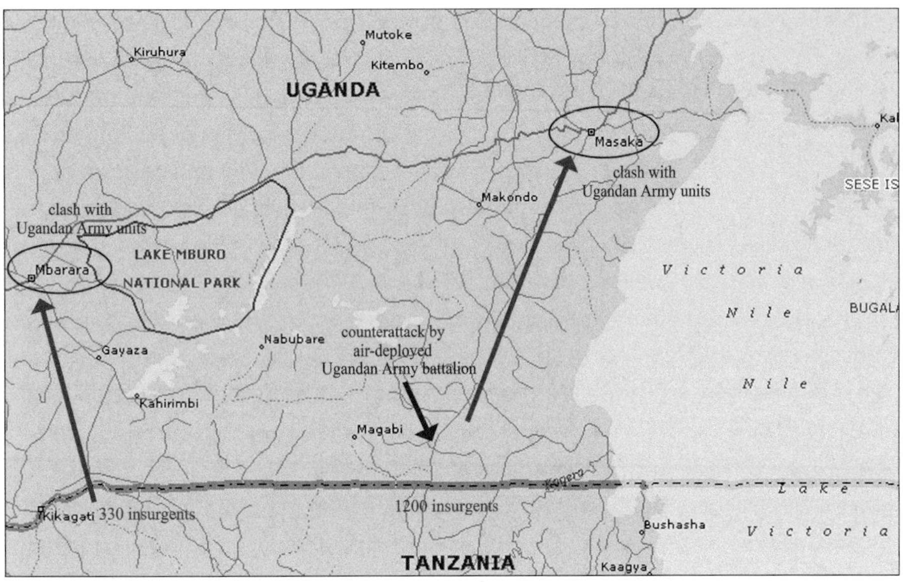

A map showing the two major prongs of the insurgent advance into southern Uganda in September 1972.

Salaam at the time that Tanzania became a beacon of progressivism in Africa. In Tanzania, Museveni met John Garang – the future leader of the Sudanese People's Liberation Movement (SPLM) – and established ties to the *Frente de Libertação de Moçambique* (Liberation Front of Mozambique, FRELIMO) – a liberation movement fighting for the independence of the Portuguese Overseas Province of Mozambique. In 1968, he organised a short trip to a FRELIMO-controlled part of Mozambique for a group of students, and a year later was invited to North Korea, where he received his first training in handling firearms. Museveni returned to Uganda in 1970 and, after Amin's coup, founded his own movement, the Front of National Salvation (FRONASA). Motivated by readings of theorists such as Mao Zedong, he intended to use FRONASA as a launching platform for a protracted insurgency that would topple the new government.[24]

By mid-1972, Obote had about 1,300 trained men and Museveni around 40. While the latter propagated a gradual escalation of guerrilla activity, the former president was in a rush and already setting up a new invasion plan. The centrepiece of the plot was an airborne assault of Entebbe IAP with the aim of disabling the UAAF MiGs, after which the commandos involved were to march on Kampala. Simultaneously, another group of insurgents was to cross the border to Uganda from the Kagera salient. Museveni reluctantly agreed to support this attempt and an invasion of Uganda was set up for 17 September 1972.[25]

On 13 September 1972, the Kenyan Directorate of Security Intelligence (colloquially known as the 'Special Branch') reported to Kampala that it had received intelligence about Tanzanian troops and Ugandan insurgents planning an invasion of Uganda. This report was dismissed and thus the attack took the government and Ugandan military by surprise.[26]The complex operation began with Obote's followers seizing a Douglas DC-9 airliner of the East African Airways company at Dar es-Salaam IAP on 15 September. This was then flown by James Lalobo – a pilot who had failed during conversion training from the Fokker F.27 to DC-9s – to an isolated airstrip near Kilimanjaro to pick up a commando force of 100 for a flight to Entebbe. However, on take-off from Dar es-Salaam, the pilot forgot to retract the undercarriage. Furthermore, on landing at Kilimanjaro, he forgot to unlock the tyre mechanism and thus burst all tyres. With the airliner in need of repairs, this part of the plan had to be abandoned.[27]

News of this failure did not reach the insurgent ground units as these were assembling at Kaboya, near Bukoba, in Tanzania and they crossed the border early on 17 September. Embarking on nine trucks, the other group of 330 insurgents (mostly armed with SAR 56 rifles, with 10 bullets per man) easily overcame a small Border-Guards unit before running into Colonel Ali Fadhul, the CO of the Mbarara-based Simba Battalion of the UA, who was alone in a white Peugeot 504. The officer reacted quickly and managed to avoid capture. Next, the column met a single UA lorry full of soldiers: these fled on sighting the insurgents, leaving behind them all their weapons and equipment. Five were captured and executed on the spot.[28] The insurgents reached Mbarara almost unopposed and destroyed the first UA Jeep they ecountered. However, immediately afterwards they were engaged by two other Army Jeeps, one carrying a general-purpose machine gun and another

Amin forcing a group of Europeans to pledge loyalty to his government in 1972. Most foreigners were soon forced to leave or felt obliged to do so. (Mark Lepko Collection)

In 1973, Amin befriended the Libyan leader Muamar el-Gaddafi. This photograph was taken during Gadaffi's visit to Kampala early that year. (Gaddafi Collection)

mounting a recoilless 106mm calibre rifle. The first shell from the latter vehicle destroyed one of the nine lorries carrying the insurgents, panicking the whole group, which fell into disarray, fled and dispersed. Many of the survivors were tracked down and killed by UA troops during the following days: only 46 insurgents in three trucks returned to Tanzania on 18 September.[29]

Another group of insurgents – led by Tito Okello and David Oyite Ojok – advanced on Masaka in a single convoy of trucks. They initially took the local UA garrison by surprise and destroyed several Jeeps that carried machine guns before continuing the advance on Kalisizo, about 19km (12 miles) away, where they ran out of ammunition. Meanwhile, UAAF transports deployed a battalion of Army troops to Lukoma airstrip, in the rear of the insurgents. During the following evening, these managed to lure the convoy into an ambush near Kiziba with the help of fake radio instructions: many of the insurgents were killed and this group disintegrated.[30] Despite this success, the government in Kampala found itself facing riots in the capital as well as in Jinja and called for assistance from Libya. On 18 September, five LAAF C-130 transports carrying a contingent of 22 Libyan Army officers and 377 troops, a group of Palestinian commanders and a consignment of arms and ammunition appeared deep inside Sudanese airspace while under way to Uganda. They were intercepted and forced to land by two Sudanese Air Force MiG-21s. Following brief negotiations, an agreement was reached for the C-130s to return to Libya. Once airborne, however, the entire Libyan formation turned around and quickly escaped into Ugandan airspace.[31] Reinforced by Libyan troops, the government then unleashed a counter-offensive against the insurgents who were still active along the border with Tanzania. On 18 September, UAAF MiG-17s and Magisters flew several attacks against various depots and roads in the area of the border town of Bukoba. These attacks were repeated on the following day, and on 22 September two UAAF MiG-17s bombed Mwanza airfield. According to contemporary media reports, nine Tanzanian civilians were killed and 11 injured.

Ugandan Army Air Force officers showing (from left to right) a MiG-17F, MiG-15UTI (serial number U606) and L-29 to members of the corps of foreign military attachés in Kampala, sometime in the early 1970s. (Albert Grandolini Collection)

These air strikes resulted in rumours that because the UAAF was left with only a few operational MiG-17s, it was a number of LAAF Mirage 5 fighter-bombers that had been deployed in Uganda; that these were manned by combat-experienced Egyptian pilots; and that these flew the above-mentioned attacks. However, no such deployments can be confirmed: the fact is that at that time the LAAF had no combat-ready Mirage pilots, while a squadron of Libyan Mirages operated by Egyptian pilots was still in training in Libya. Instead, it appears that reports of Mirages were based on the deployment of French-made Magisters of the UAAF.[32] Nevertheless, these attacks caused concerns of a counter-invasion in Dar es-Salaam: although the Tanzanian Army was deployed along the border, Nyerere called for a cease-fire.[33] With Uganda and Tanzania on the brink of war, Somali President Siad Barre quickly brokered a peace agreement – known as the Mogadishu Treaty – which was signed by foreign ministers of the two countries on 7 October. The treaty regulated the mutual withdrawal of all military forces for 18km (10 miles) from the common border, and cessation of hostile propaganda and support of any exiled opponents.[34]

Ugandan Co-operation with the Soviet Union

The near-war between Uganda and Tanzania prompted both governments to search for new sources of arms. Ironically, both countries procured armament from the Soviet Union.

As described above, Uganda had already acquired some weapons from the USSR in the mid-1960s, but immediately after the coup of 1971 co-operation between Kampala and Moscow cooled down. The situation changed in 1973, in the light of several reports broadcast by Radio Uganda alleging that a combined force of 10,000 Tanzanian Army and Ugandan insurgents had been assembled for a new invasion of Uganda. The Ugandan Army deployed its own units along the border and put the UAAF on alert. However, after reconnaissance and intelligence provided no evidence of a possible Tanzanian military build-up, no order for a pre-emptive attack was issued. Most such rumours were actually launched in order to distract attention from increasing power struggles within the Ugandan military. During the night from 23 to 24 March 1973, a six-hour battle erupted in Kampala between different ethnic groups in the Army. In May of that year, a series of arrests of UAAF officers led to a shoot-out between their supporters and security forces on the Entebbe–Kampala road.Nevertheless, after relations between Uganda and the United States deteoriorated and the US ambassador in Kampala was recalled in February 1973, a Soviet military mission visited Uganda and reached a new agreement about co-operation in November of the same year.[35] During the following two years, Amin imported arms worth US$48 million from the USSR, including combat aircraft, APCs, mortars, automatic rifles and man-portable air defence systems (MANPADs). Many thousands of Ugandans were sent for military, intelligence and technical training to the Soviet Union and other countries of the Warsaw Pact.[36] During late 1973 and 1974, the Soviets delivered 16 T-55A MBTs and 62 APCs, followed by eight MiG-21s, 100 different APCs (primarily BTR-40s) and a shipment of 9M14 Malyutka (ASCC code: AT-3 Sagger) anti-tank guided missiles (ATGMs). While Libya added a squadron of 16 British-made Saladin armoured cars, 13 additional MiGs arrived from the USSR the following year, bringing the total to 18 MiG-21MFs and at least three MiG-21UMs, together with a sizeable supply of spare parts, 850 bombs and several thousand unguided rockets of different calibre. Nine radar stations – required to support operations of manned interceptors – were set up. No less than 14 additional MiG-17s were also ordered and delivered within this deal, but Uganda never received MiG-21Fs or MiG-21F-13s, as frequently reported in the past.[37]

The Czechoslovak military mission also remained active in Uganda during this period, and was instrumental in graduating a new group of 11 pilots on L-29s on 21 November 1975. However, their contract was not extended again: due to a new rift between Kampala and Moscow, caused by a disagreement over the situation in Angola, all the Soviet and Czechoslovak instructors were sent home in late 1975 and early 1976.

A Lockheed C-130H Hercules transport in livery and markings of the Libyan Arab Air Force as in use until 1976. Five such aircraft were used to deploy a contingent of Libyan troops via Entebbe to Kampala on 18 September 1972. (Tom Cooper Collection)

A still from a video showing one of the brand-new MiG-21MFs of the UAAF making a low-altitude fly-past over Kampala, sometime in the mid-1970s. (Pit Weinert Collection)

As soon as it had enough pilots capable of converting to medium-sized transport aircraft, the JWTZ placed an order for seven DHC-4 Caribous, which were delivered in 1966 and 1967. This example – serial JW9001 – is seen during pre-delivery testing and pilot-training in Canada in 1966. (John Fricker Collection via Simon Watson)

The second batch of five DHC-4s delivered to the JWTZ in 1971 was painted in white. (Albert Grandolini Collection)

The Uganda Army Air Force's MiGs: Organisation and Insignia

Delivery of MiG-21s prompted the UAAF to establish a new unit equipped with this type of aircraft. Based at Gulu AB from 1976, it was designated 'Suicide Strike Command' and nicknamed 'Sungura', and always maintained a sizeable detachment at Entebbe IAP. The last known CO of the Sungura Squadron was Lieutenant-Colonel Ali Kiiza. Ugandan MiG-21MFs were painted 'air superiority grey', while MiG-21UMs appear to have been delivered in 'natural metal', but some were later painted in the same colour as the MiG-21MFs. These aircraft had serial numbers on their forward fuselages ranging from U901 to U919, applied in yellow and prefixed with a 'U'.Due to combat attrition, the MiG-17 Squadron was rendered largely inoperational during the final days of the war with Tanzania, but not before its last CO, Lieutenant-Colonel Andrew Mukooza, was appointed the C-in-C UAAF. Influenced by their Israeli instructors, the UAAF camouflaged its first batch of MiG-15UTIs and MiG-17Fs using a variant of the standard IDF/AF camouflage pattern. This consisted of blue (similar to RAL 5008) and brown (similar to RAL 8000) on the upper surfaces, with light grey (similar to RAL 7044) on the lower surfaces. On most photographs that show UAAF aircraft camouflaged in this way, the brown colour appears slightly lighter, sometimes almost tan, but this was probably caused by the effects of Uganda's tropical climate.There are reports that some UAAF MiG-15UTIs and MiG-17Fs wore a camouflage pattern of different colours, namely reddish-brown (similar to FS30117) and dark sand (similar to FS33351) on the upper surfaces, with lower surfaces in a shade of grey similar to the US 'neutral grey' (FS36270). This cannot be confirmed using available photographic evidence, but it is possible that all the MiG-17Fs still in service in the mid-1970s were re-camouflaged to dark grey, or dark grey and yellow sand.All MiG-15s, MiG-17s and MiG-21s had large serial numbers on their forward fuselage, applied in dark yellow and starting with the prefix 'U' (for details of known serial numbers, see the table below). MiG-17Fs painted in dark grey and yellow sand may have received serials applied in black.As well as Entebbe, Gulu and Nakasangola, the UAAF used a number of minor dirt strips in northern and north-west Uganda for temporary deployments of various aircraft. For example, it is known that three MiG-17s disabled by the Israelis at Entebbe in July 1976 were subsequently brought to Nakasangola and stored: their wreckage can be found at the same place to this day.

The original UAAF national markings consisted of a roundel with concentric rings of black, yellow, red and black, with a white centre. The white centre carried an illustration of the white-crested crane, Uganda's national emblem. Such roundels were worn in six positions – including the fin – but no roundels were ever applied on the fuselages of Ugandan MiGs. Although some other UAAF aircraft and helicopters used to feature an additional fin flash (this consisted of a total of six stripes in the Ugandan national colours, with the crane symbol in its centre), it was never applied on any MiGs during the 1960s and 1970s.

Table 3: Known serial numbers of UAAF and UPDF/AW MiGs, 1964–2009

Aircraft type	Serial number	Remarks
MiG-17F	U601	
MiG-17F	U602	
MiG-17F	U603	
MiG-17F	U604	
MiG-15UTI	U605	
MiG-15UTI	U606	
MiG-17F	U607	
MiG-17F	U614	Gate guard at Entebbe AB, 2006
MiG-15UTI	U618	Gate guard at Entebbe AB, 2007
MiG-21UM	U901	Wrecked at Entebbe, 1979, dumped at local scrap yard
MiG-21UM	U902	
MiG-21UM	U903	Wrecked at Entebbe, 1979, dumped at local scrap yard
MiG-21	U904	
MiG-21MF	U905	
MiG-21MF	U906	Wrecked at Entebbe, 1979, dumped at local scrap yard
MiG-21MF	U907	Last sighted in January 1976
MiG-21MF	U908	Wrecked at Entebbe, 1979, dumped at local scrap yard
MiG-21MF	U909	Wrecked at Entebbe, 1979, dumped at local scrap yard
MiG-21MF	U910	
MiG-21MF	U911	
MiG-21MF	U912	
MiG-21MF	U913	
MiG-21MF	U914	
MiG-21MF	U915	
MiG-21MF	U916	Damaged at Entebbe, 10 April 1979, fate unknown
MiG-21MF	U917	
MiG-21MF	U918	
MiG-21MF	U919	Wreck at Entebbe, 1995

Tanzanian Build-Up

In Tanzania, the government launched a major expansion of the JWTZ, initially ordering additional equipment from China. In 1973, it received a company each of additional Type-62 light tanks, Type-59 MBTs and Type 63 APCs. In late June of the same year, the first of an eventual 12 Shenyang F-6s fighter jets arrived, followed by up to 22 Shenyang FT-5 two-seat conversion trainers. One year later, Tanzania followed Uganda's example and began purchasing arms from Moscow. Its ground forces thus came into possession of quantities of D-30 122mm calibre howitzers, M-46 130mm calibre guns and BM-21 multiple-rocket launchers (MRLS) from Moscow. The Air Wing of the JWTZ acquired 14 MiG-21MFs and two MiG-21UMs from the USSR and at least a battalion of S-125 (ASCC code: SA-3 Goa) surface-to-air missiles (SAMs), plus associated ground support equipment including early warning radars. Although all aircraft and SAMs were stationed at Ngerengere Air Base (AB), Chinese and Soviet military personnel who supported the Tanzanian military were kept apart.Renewed tensions with Uganda prompted China to increase the aid furnished to Dar es-Salaam once again in 1976, largely through the deployment of additional advisers to the JWTZ. Because all the combat aircraft and SAMs were stationed at Ngerengere AB, Chinese instructors thus found themselves in the curious situation of having to work right next to Soviet military personnel. Tanzanians solved this by strictly segregating military contingents from these two superpowers. Otherwise, Chinese instructors working in Tanzania encountered several problems with the military discipline of the locals. For example, while Chinese officers, pilots and ground personnel spent most

A line-up of JWTZ's MiG-21s on the military apron of Mwanza airport. All aircraft (except the MiG-21UM to the left) appear to have been painted in light blue-grey and wore large serials on their front fuselages. (Omer Mees via Greg Swart)

of their service time within their bases, most JWTZ personnel would leave the base at noon to go home for lunch. At the end of the working day, most officers would leave the base to go to work in different civilian functions. Only JWTZ pilots – in particular the 11 Tanzanians trained to fly F-6s at the time – spent most of their time at Ngerengere AB.[38]

The Air Wing of the JWTZ: Organisation and Insignia

During the 1970s, the Air Wing of the JWTZ was *organised* into Kikosi cha Jeshi (KJ Brigades), three of which are known to still exist: 601 KJ controls all the aircraft and helicopters; 602 KJ is probably a technical unit; and 603 KJ operates all air defence equipment.The main bases for a unit flying fighter aircraft, known only as 'Squadron 601' were Mwanza (MiG-21s) and Ngerengere (F-6s); another brigade operated trainers, while all transport aircraft and helicopters were based at Dar-es-Salaam.Original national markings were applied in the form of roundels in four positions and a fin flash. The roundel included the stylised torch and garland applied in yellow on a green field, outlined in blue.

The first aircraft operated by the JWTZ were German-made Piaggio P.149D trainers. They received serials with the prefix 'T' (for Tanzania) and were pained in dark yellow – a colour traditionally used for training aircraft in Tanzania ever since. In 1966, a new serialling system was introduced, based on the year or delivery and starting with the prefix JW (short for *Jeshi la Wananchi*). An increased number of types in service necessitated an appropriate adaptation of this system, in 1974, to the form which is still used today. For details of both systems, see Tables 4 and 5.[39]

Table 4: JW Serialling System, 1966-1974

Prefix and first two digits	Year of delivery	Notes
JW 90xx	1966	Type 1 = DHC-4
JW 91xx	1966	Type 2 = DHC-3
JW 92xx	1966	Type 3 = P.149D
JW 93xx	1971	Type 4 = PA-28-140
JW94xx	1974	Type 5 = Cessna 310

Table 5: JW Serialling System, since 1974

Prefix and first two digits	Aircraft Type	Notes
JW 90xx	transport aircraft	Cessna 404, DHC-5 and others
JW 91xx	fighter-interceptors	F-6A, F-6C
JW 92xx	training aircraft	FT-5 (later FT-6 too)
JW 93xx	liaison aircraft	PA-28-140
JW94xx	liaison aircraft	Cessna 310
JW 95xx	light helicopters	AB.205, AB.206
JW 96xx	transport helicopters	AB.412

A still from a video showing a line-up of UAAF MiG-21s at Entebbe IAP in early 1976. The front aircraft is a MiG-21UM with serial number U901 – left unpainted in natural metal. (Albert Grandolini Collection)

Most aircraft of Chinese origin arrived in 'natural metal' and seem to have been operated in such livery during the late 1970s and for most of the 1980s. Nevertheless, some F-6s may have received a camouflage pattern consisting of sand, brick red and dark green applied on the upper surfaces and sides, and light admiralty grey on the lower surfaces. It is possible that this was applied immediately before or during the Kagera War of 1978–1979.Even less is known about Tanzania's MiG-21MFs and MiG-21UMs. They appear to have been painted in 'air superiority grey' during their service, in common with the MiG-21s later delivered to several other export customers. Four-digit serial numbers, probably in the range 92xx upwards, were applied in black or dark grey on the forward fuselage. 'JWTZ' titles were probably worn on the rear fuselage. While transport and training aircraft, and helicopters, are known to have received roundels, the only national markings on combat aircraft appear to have been the national flag, applied on the fin. This consists of elements of flags of both preceding countries (Tanganyika and Zanzibar), including green, yellow and blue fields, with a black diagonal stripe. It is possible, but remains unconfirmed, that MiG-21s of the JWTZ instead received a stylised 'Torch and Laurel Wreath' as a form of national insignia on their fins. Available photographic evidence indicates that it is possible – although by no means confirmed – that Tanzanian MiG-21s wore their full military registrations, for example JW-9221, on the fin, directly below the fin flash. Other types received four-digit serial numbers too: these were usually applied on the fins of transports and training aircraft, but on the forward fuselage of combat aircraft, always in black. Similarly, the title 'JWTZ' was applied in black on the rear fuselage of combat aircraft, and on the front of transports.

Table 6: Known serial numbers of JWTZ fighters, 1973–2009[40]

Aircraft type	Serial number	Notes
FT-5	9101	Delivered in 1973 from China
FT-5	9102	Delivered in 1973 from China; active as of 2004
FT-5	9103	Delivered in 1973 from China
FT-5	9104	Delivered in 1973 from China
FT-5	9105	Delivered in 1973 from China

FT-5	9106	Delivered in 1973 from China
FT-5	9107	Delivered in 1973 from China
FT-5	9108	Delivered in 1973 from China
FT-5	9109	Delivered in 1973 from China
FT-5	9110	Delivered in 1973 from China
FT-5	9111	Delivered in 1973 from China
FT-5	9112	Delivered in 1973 from China
FT-5	9113	Delivered in 1973 from China
FT-5	9114	Delivered in 1973 from China
FT-5	9115	Delivered in 1973 from China
FT-5	9116	Delivered in 1973 from China
FT-5	9117	Delivered in 1973 from China
FT-5	9118	Delivered in 1973 from China; active as of 2004
FT-5	9119	Delivered in 1973 from China; w/o in accident 29 June 2010
FT-5	9120	Delivered in 1973 from China; active as of 2004
FT-5	9121	Delivered in 1973 from China; active as of 2004
MiG-21UM	91??	Delivered in 1974 from USSR; stored at Mwanza since 1993
MiG-21UM	91??	Delivered in 1974 from USSR; stored at Mwanza since 1993
MiG-21UM	91??	Delivered in 1974 from USSR; stored at Mwanza since 1993
MiG-21UM	91??	Delivered in 1974 from USSR
MiG-21MF	92??	Delivered in 1974 from USSR; stored at Mwanza since 1993
MiG-21MF	92??	Delivered in 1974 from USSR; stored at Mwanza since 1993
MiG-21MF	92??	Delivered in 1974 from USSR; stored at Mwanza since 1993
MiG-21MF	92??	Delivered in 1974 from USSR; stored at Mwanza since 1993
MiG-21MF	92??	Delivered in 1974 from USSR; stored at Mwanza since 1993
MiG-21MF	92??	Delivered in 1974 from USSR; stored at Mwanza since 1993
MiG-21MF	92??	Delivered in 1974 from USSR
MiG-21MF	92??	Delivered in 1974 from USSR
MiG-21MF	92??	Delivered in 1974 from USSR
MiG-21MF	92??	Delivered in 1974 from USSR
MiG-21MF	92??	Delivered in 1974 from USSR
MiG-21MF	92??	Delivered in 1974 from USSR
F-6	9201	Delivered in 1973 from China
F-6	9202	Delivered in 1973 from China
F-6	9203	Delivered in 1973 from China; active as of 2009
F-6	9204	Delivered in 1973 from China; active as of 2009
F-6	9205	Delivered in 1973 from China; active as of 2009
F-6	9206	Delivered in 1973 from China
F-6	9207	Delivered in 1973 from China
F-6	9208	Delivered in 1973 from China
F-6	9209	Delivered in 1973 from China
F-6	9210	Delivered in 1973 from China
F-6	9211	Delivered in 1973 from China; active as of 2009
F-6	9212	Delivered in 1973 from China

The old airport terminal at Entebbe in 2009. (US DoD)

A still from a video showing UAAF MiG-21s destroyed by the Israelis at Entebbe IAP on 3 July 1976. Heavy losses of MiG-17s and MiG-21s caused by this attack prompted Amin to order another batch of MiG-21MFs from the Soviet Union. (Pit Weinert Collection)

A still of a video showing Idi Amin and two of his sons inspecting a MiG-21UM of the UAAF. (Albert Grandolini Collection)

Operation Entebbe

With the help of continuous recruiting of Nubians and Sudanese, by January 1976, the UA grew to about 19,000, including 658 officers. The air force numbered around 1,000 personnel, who operated up to 65 aircraft and helicopters.[41]

In February 1976, Amin laid claim to substantial portions of Kenya and Sudan, land that had been transferred from Uganda some 50 years earlier by the British colonial administration. Maintaining that the areas were inhabited by Ugandans and promising to protect them from 'being exploited by foreigners who are not the rightful owners of those parts', the Ugandan strongman caused a furore in Kenya and a virtual blockade of his landlocked country. Amin backed down in March, but tensions remained high and there were a series of mob attacks in both countries against each other's nationals. When Kenya demanded that all fuel shipments to Uganda be paid for in advance in foreign currency, Kampala proved unable to comply and reacted by seizing shipments destined for Rwanda, Sudan and Zaïre. Eventually, Uganda found itself forced to rely increasingly on air transportation to carry its exports and imports: goods were airlifted to Entebbe from such scattered locations as Gabon, Sudan, Djibouti and Great Britain, while coffee exports were, for the most part, routed via Djibouti and Aden by chartered aircraft (such expensive methods of shipment were justified by the extremely high level of world coffee prices).After surviving the third attempt on his life in less than a year, in early June 1976, Amin next became involved in a major international drama. On 27 June, a group of armed Palestinians hijacked an Air France Airbus A300B2 in flight from Tel Aviv to Paris. Amin granted permission for the aircraft to land at Entebbe and then took personal charge of the negotiations with the hijackers, who demanded the release of 53 Israelis in Kenyan and other prisons in other countries, was broadcast by Radio Kampala. Some 150 hostages had been released by 1 July, but 106 others were still being held captive inside the old terminal building at Entebbe IAP. Israel, meanwhile, entered into negotiations with Kampala but it soon became obvious that this was only a method of buying the time necessary to organise a rescue operation.Launched on 3 July 1976, this included four C-130 Hercules transports of the Israeli Air Force/Defence Force (IDF/AF) carrying members of the Israeli special forces, two Boeing 707 tankers and top cover provided by several F-4E Phantom IIs. These aircraft deployed from Sharm el-Sheikh airfield, in the southern Sinai, which was then under Israeli control, flying over the Red Sea to a position off the coast of Djibouti. From there, the C-130s continued over Ethiopia and arrived at Entebbe by night. Upon landing, the first Hercules disgorged a group of Israeli paratroopers and a black Mercedes sedan similar to that known to be used by Idi Amin, together with several Land Rovers. The other three C-130s followed in a similar manner, minutes later. After a brief firefight in which between 33 and 45 Ugandan soldiers, three hostages, all of the Palestinian militants and the leader of the Israeli operation were killed, hijackers brought 102 hostages to the waiting transports. Meanwhile, several Israeli operatives planted explosive devices on three nearby UAAF MiG-17s and four MiG-21s and detonated them. This action rendered most of the MiGs present at Entebbe unserviceable and thus incapable of pursuing the slow transports as they began their return journey to Israel via Nairobi, where they stopped to refuel.[42]The successful Israeli operation not only hamed Amin and the Ugandan military, but indirectly ruined whatever was left of Kampala's relations with London. One of the hostages – a 75-year-old Israeli woman who also held Brtitish citizenship – had been released by the hijackers due to illness and taken to Mulago Hospital in Kampala. After the raid, she was killed by UA officers, together with several doctors and nurses who tried to intervene.[43] Later in July, Amin went on to expell two British diplomats, while some 300 British nationals left the country fearing persecution. Finally, on 28 July, Britain announced that it was breaking diplomatic relations with Uganda.[44]While near unlimited financial assistance – and the delivery of 10 Soviet-made T-34/85 tanks – from Libya subsequently helped Amin to buy time and regain some of his popularity with the armed forces, in August he again purged many of his top commanders. Subsequently, because the Israeli raid resulted in the destruction of a sizeable part of the UAAF, Kampala requested either Libya or the Soviet Union to deliver up to a dozen new MiG-21MFs as replacements, while 30 Ugandan pilots were trained on them in the Soviet Union. Although one of the involved pilots defected to the USA shortly after returning to Uganda, the others helped establish the Suicide Strike Command – a new MiG-21-squadron, officially inaugurated at Entebbe in January 1977, and apparently including a few Palestinian pilots trained in Libya. Later the same year, a group of 10 young Ugandan women – including Amin's niece – were sent to the UK for pilot training.[45]

CHAPTER THREE:
LIBERATION WAR

In April 1978, Amin ordered another reshuffle of the UA hierarchy while establishing the Western Brigade and raising the status of the 4th Infantry Battalion to that of the Simba Mechanised Regiment. This was to be the last such action of his because his decision prompted a wave of unrest within the military. It appears that the government then attempted to distract the public's attention by spreading faulty intelligence about Tanzanians intending to invade the country. Indeed, in May of the same year, Amin ordered the UA to deploy inside the DMZ, in clear violation of the treaty from 1972. Simultaneously, reports surfaced about UAAF MiG-21s operating along the border, intercepting various light civilian aircraft and demanding their pilots to identify – but also that one of the Ugandan MiG pilots defected to the USA.[46] By early October, the situation escalated to a point where dissident troops – apparently linked to Obote and supported by Tanzania – ambushed Amin at the presidential lodge in Kampala; the president escaped with his family with the help of a UAAF helicopters. A few days later, Gen Mustafa Adrisi, Amin's Vice-President, was injured in a suspicious car accident. This prompted troops loyal to Adrisi to mutiny. Amin deployed several units – including the Simba Battalion – to crush the uprising. However, this intervention only caused additional Ugandans to flee to Tanzania. Meanwhile, rumours – all usually described as 'intelligence' – began to spread through the UA about the JWTZ preparing an invasion of Uganda. In response, Kampala officially declared war on Tanzania on 10 October 1978 and the UA's top military commanders began planning a 'preventive' attack into Tanzania. The composition of Ugandan Army units at the time is provided in Table 7.The first Ugandan troops entered Tanzania around midday on 9 October, when a motorised detachment burned two houses in Kakunyu village. The nearby JWTZ observation post called for artillery support. After one UA APC received a hit, the surviving Ugandans withdrew. On the following day, UAAF MiGs bombed the forests along the border from high altitude – without any tangible effect.At that time the Tanzanians were still in the process of training their personnel on various heavy equipment purchased in recent years from China and the Soviet Union, and were in no condition to fight a major war. The JWTZ had only one – Western – Brigade deployed within reach of Uganda, and this had only one – the 3rd – battalion protecting the border. The series of Ugandan provocations, and then the sudden Ugandan invasion, took them completely by surprise and Tanzanian troops were forced to withdraw.During the next few days, there were several exchanges of artillery fire but the situation became more serious only on 18October, when Ugandan MiGs hit the town of Bukoba, causing 'limited damage'.[47] After additional incidents, a full-scale invasion by about 2,000 UA troops – supported by tanks, APCs and artillery – was launched on 22 October.Thus began the Kagera War, a unique eight-month long conflict, the first ever in Africa to see the conventional military forces of one nation capturing the capital of another. Exploiting a perfect opportunity to hit back in force and solve its problems with Kampala once and for all, the government of Tanzania not only launched a major mobilisation and counter-attack into the Kagera Salient, but then an all-out invasion of Uganda with the intention of toppling Idi Amin's government.

Table 7: Order of Battle of Ugandan Army in October 1978

Unit	Base	Commander	Notes
1st Infantry Battalion ('Eagle Colonel Gaddafi Battalion')	Jinja		established 1960; coded 1UA; known as 'Eagle Colonel Gaddafi Battalion' under Amin
2nd Infantry Battalion ('Gondo Battalion')	Mororo	Lieutenant-Colonel Bananuka	established 1964; coded 2UA; known as 'Gondo Battalion' under Amin
3rd Infantry Battalion ('Tiger Battalion')	Mubende		established 1965; coded 3UA; known as 'Tiger Battalion' under Amin
4th Infantry Battalion ('Simba Battalion')	Mbarara		established 1965; coded 4UA; known as 'Simba Battalion' then 'Simba Mechanised Battalion/Regiment' under Amin
5th Mechanised Specialist Reconnaissance Regiment ('Suicide Regiment')	Camp Malire, Kampala; relocated to Masaka in 1971	Colonel Bernard Rwehururu	established 1967 with four mechanised companies (OT-64s), one company each of Ferret and Saladin armoured cars and two companies of tanks; known as 'Malire Mechanised Regiment'/'Suicide Regiment'/'Revolutionary Suicide Mechanised Regiment'/'Masaka Mechanised Regiment' under Amin
2nd Para Battalion	Fort Portal		established 1969; known as 'Mountain of the Moon Battalion' under Amin
Air & Sea Battalion	Tororo		
Marine Regiment	Camp Bugulobi, Kampala	Brig Taban Lupavi	including one company of OT-64s; considered most loyal to Amin (and most trusted by him)
Leopard Battalion	Gulu	Major Zziwa	established in 1972–1973 period; no alpha-numerical designation known (but often cited as 'Chui Battalion', with Chui standing for Leopard)
Military Police	Camp Makindye, Kampala		established 1967
Artillery & Signals Regiment	Masindi	Lieutenant-Colonel Abdu Kisuule	

Kagera Salient

Most Ugandan sources nowadays put the blame for outbreak of the Kagera War on Idi Amin and dissent within the UA. Some are much more precise – but also reveal quite a different flow of events, unrelated to the mutiny of Adrisi's loyalists. Abdu Kisuule, then in command of the Artillery & Signals Regiment, described the invasion as a part of a coherent plan – intending to deliver a fast and stunning blow to the Tanzanians and forcing them to accept a small territorial loss instead of undergoing a protracted war. This plot collapsed because of the indiscipline of one of the UA's top generals:

The war was to be fought on three fronts; the marine unit was to attack through Minziro Forest to Kyaka border, the Simba Regiment from Mbarara plus another four battalions from Mountains of the Moon were to advance from Nyakanyansi through Ktagata – southern front – to Kyaka Bridge, while the Malire Mechanised Regiment – supported with two other companies and three batteries from the artillery unit – was to attack via Mutukula along the Kyaka Road ... All activities were to be properly co-ordinated so that all the forces of the three prongs arrive at Bumazi at the same time ready to capture the bridge and advance to Bukoba.[48]

Also according to Kisuule, what caused the plan's downfall was Gen Juma Ali Butabika's bid to win fame and Amin's favour. Accordingly, Butabika sent his bodyguard – who was also his brother-in-law – into Tanzanian territory with the aim of capturing a Tanzanian soldier. However, the man was killed by Tanzanians and this prompted a fuming Butabika to order an invasion of Tanzania. Indeed, Bernhard Rwehururu, then serving as CO 5th Mechanised Specialist Reconnaissance Regiment (renamed 'Suicide Regiment' by Amin and including all 12 Ugandan M4A1 Shermans and T-34 tanks obtained from Libya), put all the blame on Butabika:Reports that an attack on Uganda was in the offing kept filtering into the HQs of my unit, which was also known as Suicide Headquarters. The reports incensed the foreign legions, especially the Sudanese and Congolese in the Army High Command. Led by Brigadier Malera, Taban Lupayi and Juma Butabika, they started calling for a pre-emptive attack on Tanzania. Finally, in October 1978, Juma Butabika, with a handful of some of the Malire troops, left his unit and took command of the troops that had been permanently stationed at the border before advancing into Tanzania.[49]

Whatever happened, advancing from Lukoma airstrip, two Ugandan regiment-sized task forces entered Tanzanian territory on 22 October; one led by Butabika and mounted on OT-64 APCs, supported by M4A1 Shermans, and the other led by Kisulle, consting of Jeeps carrying machine guns and recoilless rifles, additional OT-64 APCs, several T-55 MBTs and Saladin armoured cars. Advancing through banana plantations, the Ugandans reached Kabwebwe without encountering any kind of resistance. However, most of Butabika's column got struck in the mud and it was 1800 local time before its APCs were mobile again. The next morning, the furious general advanced on Bumazi but retreated at the first sign of resistance by the 3rd Battalion of the Western Brigade JWTZ, supported by a battery of 122mm howitzers and several 85mm cannons. Indeed, Ugandan radio messages intercepted by Tanzanian military intelligence indicated that involved UA units were quite confused and had no clue about how weak the Tanzanian units on the border were.[50] Nevertheless, with only minimal ammunition reserves, the 3rd Battalion was soon forced to withdraw south of the Kagera River. Rwehururu commented rather optimistically:

The attack took the few ill-equipped Tanzanian troops stationed at Mutukula and Minziro by surprise and they fled the area. Encouraged by the lack of resistance, Butabika[,] who claimed to have been in Masaka by accident, rang Amin, claiming that Tanzanian troops had made an incursion into Uganda, prompting him to take command at the border guard in order to repulse the invaders ... Amin fell for the lie, largely because it presented an opportunity for him to annex chunks of Tanzanian territory. He speedily sanctioned Butabika's southward march to Kyaka Bridge though Kasambya. Through the troops did not cross the Kyaka Bridge, they had effectively sealed off the entire Kagera Salient and on 1 November, Amin went on air and announced that his government had annexed the Kagera Salient.

Towards the end of his bizarre rule over Uganda, Idi Amin could hardly find any place for all the decorations on his uniform. (Pit Weinert Collection)

A pair of T-55As on a parade in Kampala in early 1978. By that time a company of MBTs of this type should have been assigned to the 4th Infantry Battalion, enabling its expansion into the 'Simba Mechanised Regiment'. (Albert Grandolini Collection)

Get the Fighting Started

Although the CO of the Western Brigade JWTZ, Brig Yusuf Hamid, had been warning about Ugandan provocations – including reconnaissance flights of UAAF Cessnas into Tanzanian airspace – since July 1978, when the UA crossed the border the 3rd Battalion was still the only Tanzanian military unit deployed in the area. Its HQ was at Kyaka, on the southern side of the Kagera River, 30km from Uganda.[51] Contrary to other reports, the JWTZ had no two

A still from a video showing Idi Amin with the crew of an OT-64A APC, somewhere in southern Uganda, in 1978. (Albert Grandolini Collection)

Another still from the same video, this time showing Amin riding one of the Ugandan M4 Shermans. The vehicle in question was of particular interest for wearing full markings of the 5th Mechanised 'Suicide' Regiment, including green and red quadrants applied on the front and sides of the hull. (Albert Grandolini Collection)

additional brigades nearby: out of its three other brigades, only the Southern Brigade – headquartered in Songea, in south-western Tanzania, nearly 1,100km away from Uganda, with no roads or railroads in between – was considered operational and combat ready. Because it took days for that unit to reach the Kagera Salient, the only reinforcement for the 3rd Battalion the JWTZ was able to deploy immediately consisted of a six-member team equipped with 9K32 Strela (SA-7) man-portable air defence systems (MANPADs), which arrived in Kyaka on 28 October.The reason for the deployment of the latter unit was activity by Ugandan MiGs, which flew several strikes on Bukoba and Kagera Bridge on 21 and 27 October. While some of their bombs fell into Lake Victoria and others hit nearby forests, one 125kg calibre weapon exploded 50 metres from Bukoba hospital, shattering the building's windows. Although there were no casualties, all civilians subsequently fled the town. Attacks on Kagera Bridge were much less successful, as light bombs and rockets proved ineffective against its construction.[52] Ugandan MiGs returned to the skies over Tanzania on the morning of 28 October, but by then the JWTZ SA-7 team took up positions near the HQ of the 3rd Battalion in Kyaka. After waiting for several hours for UAAF fighter jets to approach within range, the team fired one missile which scored a direct hit on the MiG-21 flown by Major Omita. The Ugandan pilot ejected safely and parachuted into dense forest, making good his escape towards the positions of friendly troops. Acknowledging the loss, the Ugandan government extended claims for a number of JWTZ fighters shot down, noting that its jets had 'routed a Tanzanian air attack headed for major Ugandan cities'.[53]

By the morning of 30 October, JWTZ intelligence concluded that 'thousands' of Ugandan troops had entered the Kagera Salient along the axis Kakunga-Masanya-Mutukula, and at Minzero. Despite a cautious advance, they covered the 30km to the Kagera River and Kyaka Bridge by that evening before halting. Contrary to Tanzanian expectations, the UA failed to continue its advance on Kyaka, although this was only lightly defended. Later the same day, a worried Nyerere held a meeting with his top commanders, including Lieutenant Gen Abdallah Twalipo (Minister of Defence), Major-Genaral Tumanie Kiwelu (Chief of Staff JWTZ and commander of all units facing Uganda) and Lieutenant-Colonel Gore (Christian Kakwa, recently appointed CO Air Wing JWTZ). In the course of this conference, Twalipo assured that the military was able to expel the invaders, but added that it would take some time until the JWTZ would be able to mount a major operation to liberate the Kagera Salient. Twalipo and Kiwelu planned to fight the war in two phases. During the first, which was to start immediately, they intended to liberate the Kagera Salient by the end of January 1979. In the second phase, they planned a shallow invasion in order to enable Ugandan insurgents to advance on Kampala and topple Idi Amin. Reassured, Nyerere ordered him to 'get started'.On 2 November, the Southern Brigade was ordered to re-deploy all of its 4,000 troops, tanks and artillery to the border with Uganda. Reinforcements in form of elements from the Western Brigade (HQ in Tabora) were to follow.[54]

Tanzanian Lieutenant-Colonel Lupembe was then in command of a battalion of troops preparing for deployment in Namibia under the UN peacekeeping mission. He recalled the deployment of his unit to the combat zone with help of JWTZ Caribous:While at Makambaku base where I was preparing my battalion, I got a message from the MOD asking me to go to Mbeya … I mobilised transport to Mbeya where I was told we were to be airlifted to a destination only known by the pilots … We were airlifted to Tabora, where I met Gen Kiwelu, who was the chief planner and commander of the forces preparing to force the Ugandan Army out of Tanzanian territory.[55]

Tanzanian Counter-offensive

On 1 and 2 November 1978, the UAAF continued dispatching MiGs to hit the Kyaka Bridge. Because Amin had disbanded the Engineer Corps in 1972, the Army proved unable to blow up this structure. As the Army failed to advance over the bridge, the JWTZ SA-7 team took up positions on the southern bank and opened fire at the MiGs, claiming several of them as shot down. Another air strike on Kyaka Bridge was flown on 3 November, again without success, prompting Rwehururu into the following comments:

Butabika and his men – ignorant of military amphibious operations and

A column of JWTZ infantry advancing along one of the few hardened roads in the country. At the time of the Ugandan invasion, the Tanzanian military was ill-prepared for a war; the Army had its units in different states of build-up and readiness, scattered all over the country, and had to rush them over hundreds of kilometres to the battlefield. (Albert Grandolini Collection)

the availability of [an] emergency pontoon bridge – asked Amin to sanction air raids on the bridge. Approval was immediately given, but the inadequate firepower and poor marksmanship of our jet pilots meant that it was only after ballistic experts from Kilembe mines were ordered in, that the bridge was finally blown up, sparking off wild celebrations.[56]

After this action, the UA's advance into Tanzania was completely stopped. The Ugandans failed to secure the Taka Bridge and after the destruction of the Kyuka Bridge could not advance over the Kagera River due to the lack of equipment for amphibious operations. Meanwhile, in their rush to mobilise and bring as many troops as possible to the front line, Tanzanians were also to experience a nasty incident. On 3 November, the Air Wing JWTZ decided to deploy a squadron F-6 jets to Mwanza. Constructed directly on the shores of Lake Victoria, Mwanza was only 150km (93 miles) away from the border with Uganda and 280km (174 miles) from Entebbe AB, and therefore the closest airfield to the theatre of operations. This deployment ended in an early catastrophe. While descending over the town of Musomo, the fighters entered the airspace protected by the SA-3 battalion of the Air Defence Command JWTZ, which had been deployed in the area only recently. Along with this unit, at least a battery of anti-aircraft artillery opened fire too. The F-6 flown by Ayekuwa Akiirusha was hit first and shot down, killing its pilot. Another jet crashed after running out of fuel some 50km (31 miles) away from Mwanza, after its pilot ejected safely. Short of fuel and unable to divert to another airfield, other pilots braved the heavy anti-aircraft fire.[57] A subsequent investigation revealed that there had been a grievous mistake within the chain of command, and nobody had informed locally-based units of the decision to deploy F-6s to Mwanza. As a result, air defences misidentified the F-6s as Ugandan MiGs about to attack the airfield and opened fire.

Undeterred by this shattering loss, Major-Genaral Kiwelu took over the overall command of Tanzanian forces along the Kagera River. Although the two brigades deployed from other parts of the country were still on the march – slowed down by unusually heavy rains that transformed most of the 'roads' between Bukoba and Kyaka into a sea of mud – he already began issuing orders for a counter-offensive. For this purpose, JWTZ artillery began fierce shelling of the northern bank of Kagera on 14 November, while engineers started assembling a Chinese-made pontoon bridge and clearing minefields they had constructed during the retreat just a few weeks earlier. Having failed to dig trenches, Ugandan units deployed along the Kagera River took casualties and broke, fleeing back towards the border and then in the direction of Mutukula. They were pursued by several long-range patrols of the JWTZ which on 22 November not only reached the border with Uganda, but reported encountering no Ugandan troops inside the salient, except for, 'two tanks and 30 soldiers'.[58] Instead of securing the area under their control, most Ugandan officers and their troops were busy celebrating a 'victory': drinking, looting, gang raping and murdering the local population. According to Tanzanian sources, not only did they take away everything they could carry from the Kagera Salient, but they also murdered more than 1,500 civilians. Rwehururu explained the situation as follows:

Intelligence reports indicating Tanzania was building up positions started trickling in. We duly passed them on to our superiors in Masaka, but none of these reports was taken seriously. It was then that I realised that since the people on the ground were not taking the reports seriously, the Uganda Prisons Services corporal-cum-tractor-driver who had become the Chief of Staff would not react to those reports with the seriousness they deserved.

Unsurprisingly, when three JWTZ brigades used another pontoon bridge (a Bailey-type construction purchased from Britain that enabled the transfer of tanks and trucks towing artillery) to launch a general attack into the flank of Ugandan units in the Kagera Salient on 23 November, they encountered next to no resistance. Tanzanians recovered the area within only two days at the cost of just a few fatalities caused in traffic accidents.Amid the chaos and panic on the Ugandan side, few officers took their jobs seriously enough to call for air strikes on Tanzanian pontoon bridges and advancing ground troops. Only four MiG-21s are reliably confirmed to have appeared over the combat zone. Two hit the dirt landing strip in Bukoba, but caused negligible damage. Two others attacked the Mwanza airfield, but encountered heavy anti-aircraft fire and both were hit. Lieutenant Nobert Atiku was forced to eject from his stricken aircraft and became one of the first Ugandan prisoners of war (POWs) in Tanzania. The other MiG, flown by Captain Kiiza (apparently one of the few Ugandans trained in Israel who still served with the UAAF), was

Aiming to replace its tired DHC-4s, the JWTZ placed an order for six more advanced DHC-5s in 1978. The first four of these arrived in the same year. This example (serial JW9021) is seen during pre-delivery testing in Canada. (Albert Grandolini Collection)

hit by an SA-7 in the tail section but remained airborne. Kiiza flew the badly-damaged aircraft to a safe emergency landing at Entebbe AB. He was subsequently promoted in rank to major and appointed CO of the sole UAAF MiG-21 squadron.[59] Ironically, despite this failure and although the JWTZ is not known to have flown any kind of air raids into Tanzania before April 1979, Kampala subsequently boasted about 'routing' another Tanzanian attack heading for major Ugandan cities.

Expansion of the JWTZ

In early December 1978, Nyerere and his military commanders found themselves facing a dilemma of what to do next. While the swift recovery of the Kagera Salient convinced them that the UA was no match for the JWTZ, it was obvious that the victory provided no security from Amin's bizarre style of government. This led to the conclusion that a counter-invasion of Uganda was necessary. Despite the obvious necessity of such an action, such aggression against a neighbouring country was likely to cause fierce international criticism, perhaps even diplomatic isolation, which Tanzania could ill-afford. Eventually, although facing severe international pressure, Nyerere and Kiwelu were emboldened by support they began receiving from Algeria (which discretely sent three shipments of arms), Angola, Ethiopia, Mozambique and Zambia, and decided their advance into Uganda should remain limited in scope: the JWTZ was to capture the high ground around the town of Mutukula, which dominated the border area, followed by the towns of Mbarara and Masaka, extracting revenge for the destruction in the Kagera Salient.It would then allow an advance on Kampala by the Ugandan insurgents, the leaders of which were promising to trigger a popular uprising.[60]

By late 1978, there was a huge number of organisations of exiled Ugandans in Tanzania. The biggest of these was gathering around Milton Obote, including about 800 trained combatants organised into the Special Battalion commanded by Colonel Tito Okello. Just like in 1972, another contingent of Ugandan exiles came from Museveni's FRONASA. Although still a relatively small group, this organisation enjoyed the support of Nyerere's government – not only because it was considered an ideological ally, but because the Tanzanian government saw it as a tool of preventing the complete domination of Obote's UPC over the Ugandan political landscape.[61]Meanwhile, the JWTZ was significantly expanded and its ground forces completely reorganised. Mobilisation of all reserves increased the total available manpower from around 40,000 to nearly 150,000 (including about 40,000 members of the NPC militias which were integrated into regular JWTZ units) and enabled the establishement of dozens of new battalions and brigades, all of which received numerical designations. Steven Isaac Mtemihonda described the process of the establishment of one of these new units as follows:

Because of their heavy use for hauling troop reinforcements and supplies into the combat zone, nearly all the JWTZ's DHC-4s received a disruptive camouflage pattern in three colours on their top surfaces and sides. This example has the serial number JW9014 (serials of Tanzanian DHC-4s were in the range from JW9001 up to JW9015). (Albert Grandolini Collection)

Wreckage of Maj Omita's MiG-21, shot down by SA-7s during an attack on Kyaka on 28 October 1978. (via Martin Smisek)

> *When the war began in 1978, I was in Arusha, serving as a major and deputy battalion commander, preparing for the annual military activities of our brigade. We had just started our exercise when the news of [the] invasion of Kagera came … I was promoted to a Lieutenant-Colonel and appointed a battalion commander (in our system, a battalion is commanded by a Lieutenant-Colonel). Since my unit was already assembled, orders came from the MOD in Dar es-Salaam for my unit to move to Kagera. When the battalion went there, my brigade commander thought there would be need for more troops. I was sent to Tanga to form and train a new battalion. This was the same battalion with which I joined the war in 1979: the 21st, assigned to the 205th Brigade commanded by Brig Ramadhani Haji (replaced by Brig Herman Lupogo and then by Brig Muhidin Kimario).*[62]

In all, the JWTZ deployed five brigades – the 201, 205, 206, 207 and 208 (former Southern Brigade), each controlling up to seven infantry battalions, platoons of tanks and several artillery

As well as a team equipped with SA-7 MANPADs, the JWTZ deployed three batteries of these Chinese-made Type-55 37mm calibre anti-aircraft cannons between Kyaka and Mwanza. This combination was usually sufficient to prevent Ugandan MiG pilots from aiming accurately. (Albert Grandolini Collection)

President Julius Nyerere (centre) with two of his top military commanders during the early part of the war with Uganda of 1978–1979. (Albert Grandolini Collection)

A Tanzanian Type-62 light tank during a parade in the mid-1970s. It seems that by the time of the war with Uganda, most of these tanks had lost their large turret insignia. Despite its thin armour and light armament, the Type-62 proved mechanically reliable and offered invaluable service during this conflict. (Albert Grandolini Collection)

batteries – along the border with Uganda. Furthermore, the F-6 squadron deployed at Mwanza was reinforced by the MiG-21 squadron, and both units flew regular combat air patrols (CAPs) along the border.The UPC, FRONASA and other contingents of Ugandan exiles were initially operating independently. However, in mid-January 1976, two of the groups in question launched an attempt to cross Lake Victoria and attack Kampala in the hope of prompting local military units to mutiny against Amin. This effort ended when one of their overcrowded boats capsized and 82 insurgents drowned. Subsequently, all the Ugandan elements – about 2,000 combatants in total – were concentrated within the newly-established Uganda National Liberation Army (UNLA). However, although nominally organised into battalions and – on 21 March 1979 – the Minziro Brigade, the UNLA never operated as a cohesive body but was distributed as found suitable by Tanzanians. For example, one of its first battalions, about 600 (later 800) men under the command of Colonel Ojok, was destined to fight in central and eastern Uganda, while the other, commanded by Colonel Okello, was assigned to 206 Brigade JWTZ.[63]All Tanzanian and Ugandan units were put under the command of Major-Genaral David Msugiri, an old hand who used to serve with the King's African Rifles and fought in the Second World War. Kiwelu, who was meanwhile working 20 hours a day, was thus finally free to return to Dar es-Salaam and resume his duties as Chief of Staff.[64]

Saba-Saba

Because the JWTZ was preoccupied with its expansion and reorganisation, only a few minor clashes along the border between Uganda and Tanzania took place during December 1978, in the course of which Tanzanians claimed the destruction of a few enemy MBTs and APCs. The relative inactivity of the Tanzanian military lulled Amin and his top commanders into feeling safe. Only the crack Suicide Mechanised Specialist Reconnaissance Regiment was deployed in the field, its elements entrenching themselves on the high ground around Mutukulla. Similarly, except for flying a few patrols along the border, the UAAF entirely missed the chance to disturb the JWTZ's deployment and preparations; scared by the threat of SAMs and interceptors, it never attacked any of the many lengthy columns of Tanzanian military moving along roads from the south towards Bukoba, Kayanga and Katoro, and from there further north.Therefore, it came as a big surprise for Ugandans when, on 25 December, Tanzanians opened vicious artillery fire on Ugandan positions. Making extensive use of BM-21 MRLS, they especially targeted positions of the Artillery & Signals Regiment, soldiers of which were shocked by the appearance of this new weapon they nicknamed Saba-Saba, as described by Abdu Kisuule:

On Christmas Day of 1978, they started using the Saba-Saba rocket launchers. That day alone they hit 12 of my posts. I will never forget that day. Launching their rockets from [the] Tanzanian side, Julius Nyerere['s] men hit the bridge connecting Kakuuto with Mutukula. They hit us so much that I ran away from Lukoma airstrip to [an]other place.

It was only by sheer stroke of luck – when one of the rockets failed to detonate after hitting Ugandan positions – that the UA discovered the nature of this weapon. Rocket firing went on for days, and then weeks, as recalled by Rwehururu:

The shelling went on for weeks, seriously affecting the morale of my men. It was then we requested air support against the mysterious Saba Saba artillery, the idea being to locate and destroy it. But the enemy

While Ugandan Army units quickly fell back due to Tanzanian counter-attacks, UAAF MiGs continued bombing targets in northern Tanzania for several days. This MiG-21MF (serial number U907) is deploying its airbrakes in order to slow down for landing at Entebbe in the mid-1970s. (Tom Cooper Collection)

A memorial for JWTZ F-6-pilot Ayekuwa Akiirusha, shot down and killed during deployment to Mwanza airfield on 3 November 1978. (via Pit Weinert)

acquired SAM-7s that harassed and destroyed some of the MiG fighter jets dispatched for the operation. The mission aborted. We remained in our trenches, waiting for divine intervention.

Although sources are unclear in this regards, it seems that at least one of the two MiG-21s sent to bomb Tanzanian MRLS positions outside Bukoba was shot down by SA-7s, some time in mid-January 1979.

Eradication of Mutukula

After launching rocket attacks on Ugandan positions in the Mutukula area for nearly a month, Tanzanians launched their ground attack on 21 January 1979, at 2200 local time, in a heavy downpour. During the night, several infantry battalions of 208 Brigade approached Ugandan positions around the town and began infiltrating them. Meanwhile, a battalion led by Lieutenant-Colonel Salim Hassan Boma – supported by a few tanks – made a diversion by advancing straight on Mutukula along the road from the border. The Ugandans opened fire at this unit, but were distracted when Tanzanian infantry attacked them from the rear, and they broke and ran, leaving behind most of their armament and ammunition – but not before claiming to have killed 'hundreds' of the enemy.[65] Inside Mutukula, troops of 208 Brigade ran into a platoon of Ugandan tanks. After one of the Shermans was knocked out, the others quickly withdrew. The town was thus overrun within only six hours, and the 'crack' Suicide Regiment ran away after losing 14 troops killed in action (KIA). According to Tanzanian sources, the JWTZ destroyed one and captured another Ugandan tank, destroyed three OT-64 APCs and captured three 120mm calibre mortars and three 160mm calibre mortars, for the loss of three KIA and several dozen wounded in action (WIA).[66]This operation ended in particularly bitter fashion. Furious over Ugandan atrocities against the population of the Kagera Salient, Tanzanian troops then destroyed Mutukula: while the population was summarily executed, bulldozers levelled all the buildings. The town was literally eradicated from the map by noon on 22 January. Angry at the massacre, Nyerere reacted by issuing strict orders for the military to protect all civilians and their property. Not only commanders but also political commissaries (attached to the commander of each of the JWTZ's brigades) were personally responsible for any misconduct of their troops.[67]

Battle of Simba Hills

Instead of reacting to this catastrophe by deploying reinforcements and supplies to the border, Amin and members of the Army High Command were busy celebrating the eighth anniversary of Amin's rule. The only unit sent to reinforce the Suicide Regiment in southern Uganda was the 1st Infantry Battalion UA, which was ordered to defend Sanje. The JWTZ was thus left with all the time it needed to regroup its units and let its engineers construct a dirt strip outside Mutukula, enabling transport aircraft to deliver ammunition, reinforcements and supplies directly to the front line. It was during the following lull in the fighting that such elements of Tanzanian forces as the newly-established 205 Brigade, but also the FRONASA contingent (which meanwhile grew to between 80 and 90 combatants), reached the battlefield. The latter was used to serve as scouts for 206 Brigade JWTZ – a powerful formation commanded by Lieutenant-Colonel Mayunga, consisting of six battalions deployed for an advance into western Uganda.[68]The Tanzanians resumed their offensive in mid-February, once they felt everything was ready and in place. Major-Genaral Msugiri's main force – the 20th Division that included the 201, 207 and 208 Brigades – advanced on Sanje with the intention of reaching the Simba Hills and the town of Masaka. Msugiri's plan called for the 201 and 208 to attack from the south-west, while the 207 would hit the Ugandan flank from the east. However, during the march the scouts of the 207 stumbled into a concentration of about 500 UA troops supported by APCs and MBTs stationed at Katera Peninsula in the swampy Sango Bay of Lake Victoria. Unable to ignore this group in his rear, Msugiri ordered the 207 to attack. Studying the

Two Type-62 light tanks, a Land Rover and JWTZ infantry during their advance into Uganda in late 1978. Even the best units of the Ugandan Army proved no match for Tanzanian troops. (Albert Grandolini Collection)

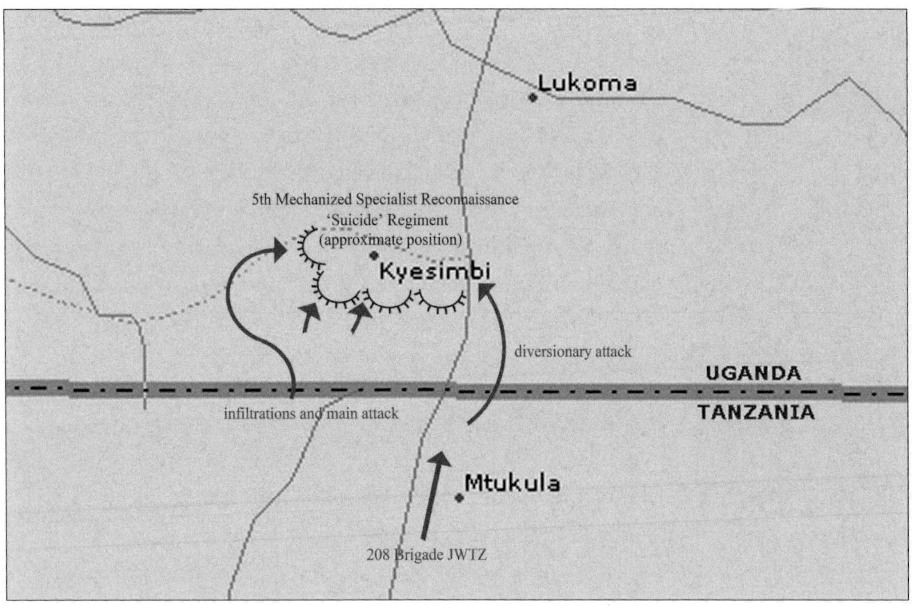

A map of the Battle of Mutukula, fought on 21 and 22 January 1979, in the course of which 208 Brigade JWTZ destroyed most of the 5th Mechanised 'Suicide' Regiment UA and forced its remnants to withdraw towards the north. (Tom Cooper)

map of the area, the commander of this unit, Brig John Walden, decided his troops should approach the enemy position along a narrow footpath through the swamp instead of along the main road, which would have positioned them right in front of Amin's tanks. Moving in a single file, soldiers often had to wade in shoulder-deep water and overcame swarms of insects, while most of their rations and ammunition became wet and spoiled. Nevertheless, they advanced 36km (22 miles) in only 50 hours, earning themselves the nickname the 'Amphibious Brigade'. Following a few hours of rest, the 207 assaulted Katera with support from an artillery barrage – only to find the Ugandan positions abandoned.[69] Meanwhile, the 201 and 208 approached the Simba Hills, infiltrating their elements around enemy flanks to block all possible avenues of retreat. Their assault was launched on 11 February, with artillery support, and encountered only sporadic resistance, primarily by those soldiers of the 1st Infantry Battalion UA who felt trapped. In just two days, Tanzanians captured Kikanda, Nsambya and Simba Hill, killing between 100 and 200 Ugandan troops in the process (only those at Nsambya Hill were partially entrenched), capturing six intact T-55s, three OT-64s and a dozen artillery pieces, before continuing to secure the Lukoma airstrip further west.[70]

Due to this Tanzanian operation receiving sporadic support from MiGs of the Air Wing JWTZ, and because Ugandan MiGs attempted several times to bomb advancing JWTZ troops, the battle saw some of most intensive aerial activity of the war, resulting in Tanzanian claims for no less than 19 UAAF aircraft shot down. While no details were ever released, it seems that the Tanzanian SA-7 teams proved most successful. On 14 February, two UAAF MiG-21s attempted to bomb the airstrip in Lukuma but without success; the site was not only well defended, but Tanzanian MiG-pilots eagerly protected the activity of their transport aircraft that continued hauling ammunition and fuel to the front lines. Therefore, the Ugandans beat a hasty retreat.[71]

Battles of Mbarara and Masaka

The western prong of the Tanzanian offensive – that on Mbarara – meanwhile encountered serious resistance. Advancing over hilly terrain and along twisting roads, advance elements of 206 Brigade – a unit largely composed of NPC militia – ran into a Ugandan rearguard in Gayaza, about 45km north of the border, and lost two tanks to bazookas. When the 20th Battalion (CO Lieutenant-Colonel N. D. Nshimani) launched a pursuit of retreating Ugandan troops, it fell into a well-laid ambush of the 'Mountains of the Moon' (or 2nd Para) Battalion UA, and suffered a loss of 24 KIA. It took Myanga a full day to deploy two other battalions behind the Ugandan position and overcome it. Unsurprisingly, henceforth his brigade advanced in a much more cautious fashion.[72]

On 20 Februrary, the JWTZ launched a pre-dawn attack from three directions on Kalisizo, some 28km (17 miles) south of Masaka. Ugandan defences – including about 600 troops of the 1st Infantry Battalion – crumbled, survivors fleeing in the direction of Masaka while leaving more than 200 KIA on the battlefield. With this, the Tanzanians reached good positions to assault their actual objective – assumed to have been defended by 'thousands' of Ugandan troops (including the Suicide Regiment) under the command of Brig Isaac Malyamungu – but instead of continuing to advance, the JWTZ was ordered to stop and replenish again, pending a meeting of the Organisation of African Unity (OAU). Exploiting the opportunity, Malyamungu's units launched several probes against Tanzanian positions, but all were repulsed. In return, the Tanzanian artillery fired nearly 1,000 shells into the town during the evening of 23

February. While primarily targeting the barracks of the Suicide Regiment, the Tanzanians were not particularly concerned about hitting civilians: they knew that most of the population had fled already because of atrocities by the UA, members of which remained liable to loot, murder and rape at every opportunity.The next morning, Major-Genaral Msugiri unleashed his attack and 201 and 208 Brigade quickly accomplished their task against next to no resistance. Subsequently, the JWTZ received the order to destroy the town and all the surviving buildings were levelled with the help of explosives.[73]

On the western side of the Tanzanian advance, 206 Brigade captured Mbarara on 25 February, following a short clash between the FRONASA contingent and the 'Simba' (or 4th Infantry) Battalion UA – supposedly Amin's best troops. Lupembe described the advance on this town as follows:

While heading for Mbarara, we learned of the presence of the Simba Unit … Our plan was to encircle Mbarara, but then a member of FRONASA told us there was a river passing by the town and we could not encircle it. Instead, we decided to enter the town across the bridge. This had to be secured first, of course. Fortunately, the bridge was not defended by Amin's men: we crossed over easily, entered Mbarara and then spread in different places in the town … the Simba Battalion had run away.

As in Masaka, the empty town was then levelled by a combination of artillery shelling and explosives.The sole Ugandan response to Tanzanian success was again the UAAF. On 27 February, four MiG-21s attacked the airstrip in Mutukula, but no less than three were claimed as shot down by JWTZ SA-7s, witgh one pilot captured after ejecting safely. It was within the context of such operations that the MiG-21s of the two air forces clashed for the only time in the course of this war, sometime in early March. Except for the outcome, all other circumstances of the resulting air battle are unknown: a Ugandan MiG-21 was hit and crashed near Byesika village, 5km (3 miles) from the Masaka–Mubende road, killing its pilot. The successful JWTZ pilot remains unknown.[74]

New Objective: Phase Three

As described above, Tanzanian leaders originally planned to end their invasion after capturing Masaka and Mbarara. However, contrary to promises given by their Ugandan allies, this success triggered no popular uprising or any kind of mutiny against Amin within the UA. Although the majority of the local population showed support for the Tanzanian invasion, Ugandan exiles – especially Obote's UPC – proved much less successful in recruiting volunteers than expected.[75]

The FRONASA – which was given the ruins of Mbarara (Museveni's home town) as a new base and recruiting centre – managed to attract around 2,000 recruits, but it was clear that it would be months before these could be trained into a coherent military force. On the contrary, experiences from after the 1971 and 1972 Ugandan-Tanzanian confrontations had shown that Amin's government was likely to savagely avenge its defeat on the population of southern Uganda if the JWTZ pulled out. Therefore, and although embarrassed by being called an 'aggressor' by various statesmen of the OAU, and suffering from diplomatic complications, Nyerere was left with no solution but to order the JWTZ to prepare for Phase Three of the war: an advance on Kampala.Before this, the Tanzanian generals again reorganised their forces. A study of the terrain further north of their positions made it clear that one force would have to advance well into western Uganda, quite isolated from the forces of the 20th Division, the main objective of which became Kampala. This prompted the JWTZ to give the western force a great deal of autonomy: the Minziro Brigade and the 206 formed the Task Force commanded by Silas Myunga, who was promoted to major general for this purpose. Henceforth, the organisation of Tanzanian – and Ugandan exile – units in Uganda was as provided in Table 8.

Table 8: Order of Battle of the Tanzanian People's Defence Forces, March 1979

Operational Group	Brigade	Commander	Notes
20th Division		Major-Genaral David Msugiri	
	201 Brigade	Brig Imran Komba	composed of NPC-units until Battle of Lukaya; mixed with regulars afterwards
	203 Brigade	Brig Muhiddin Kimario	deployed in Uganda after fall of Kampala; 14th Battalion
	205 Brigade	Brig Herman Lupogo	21st, 80th Battalion, Special Forces Battalion
	207 Brigade	Brig John 'Black Mamba' Walden	
	208 Brigade	Brig Mwita Marwa	ex-Southern Brigade; 17th, 18th, 19th Battalions; Brigade Task Force & Special Forces Battalion; reinforced by 7th and 24th Battalions after the fall of Kampala
Task Force		Major-Genaral Silas Myunga	former CO 206 Brigade
	206 Brigade	Brig Roland Makunda	ex-Western Brigade; 2nd, 20th, 25th, 79th Battalions, Brigade Task Force & Special Forces Battalion
	Minziro Brigade	Brig Ahmed Kitete	

Libyan Intervention

Facing the JWTZ's presence in Uganda there were still significant contingents of the UA. Although driven out of its home base in Mbarara, the Simba Regiment established defensive positions north of that town, from where it began shelling the Tanzanians. This position was soon reinforced by detachment from the Mountains of the Moon Regiment. In the east, the brigades assigned to the 20th Division JWTZ found themselves facing a major obstacle in form of a 20-km (12-mile) causeway stretching from Nabusanke in the north to Lukaya (a town about 31km north of Massaka)

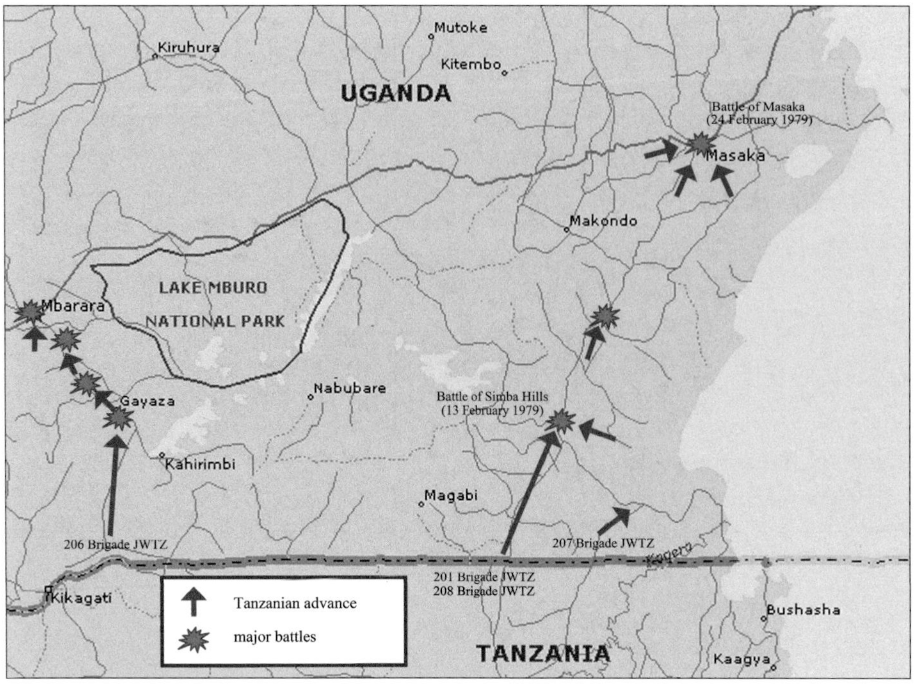

A map showing the first phase of the Tanzanian advance into Uganda, with attacks in the direction of Mbarara and Masaka. (Tom Cooper)

Troops of 208 Brigade JWTZ take a rest after the capture of Mutukula in late January 1979. Consisting of seasoned professionals, this unit was to repeatedly prove its value during the Ugandan-Tanzanian War. (Albert Grandolini Collection)

A GAZ-64 'Jeep' of the JWTZ in the late 1960s. Even in 1978–1979, the Tanzanian military was critically short of suitable vehicles and thus most of its infantry had to march not only to the front lines but also all the way from the border with Uganda to Kampala and further north. (Albert Grandolini Collection)

in the south. Because the surrounding swamp was too deep to move any vehicles through, there was no way of avoiding this causeway: it had to be secured, although it was easily defendable from the solid ground at its northern terminus. Indeed, Tanzanian intelligence indicated that whatever was left of the Suicide Regiment and the Artillery & Signals Regiment was already entrenching near Nabusanke and in the process of receiving major reinforcements.Although nearly ignored in Kampala, the successful Tanzanian invasion and series of Ugandan defeats was elsewhere recognised as a clear threat to Amin's government. Determined to help what he understood as an 'Islamic republic being invaded by a Christian army', Libyan leader Gaddafi ordered his military to launch an intervention. During the second half of February, the LAAF began a major airlift to Entebbe, using C-130 Hercules transports to deploy 2,500 troops of the Libyan People's Militia and members of the Islamic Pan-African Legion, supported by a company of 15 T-55 MBTs, 12 BM-21 MRLs, two batteries of D-30 howitzers and dozens of Land Rovers mounting recoilless 106mm calibre rifles of the Libyan Arab Army (LAA). Libyans also flew in plenty of supplies and ammunition.[76] Whether the LAAF deployed some of its MiG-21s or Mirage 5s in Uganda, as sometimes reported, remains unknown: what is certain is that a corresponding movement of such short-ranged aircraft would have been sighted and reported, as they would have to make plenty of refuelling stops while travelling from Libya to Uganda. Indeed, even the much longer-ranged Hercules transports had to refuel in Nairobi while underway to Entebbe. Nevertheless, it is confirmed that at least two (according to other sources, four) LAAF Tu-22 bombers arrived at Nakasangola AB, in northern Uganda, sometime in early March.[77]

Tanzanians monitored the Libyan deployment with increasing concern, but did not receive intelligence about the first contingent of Libyan troops – including most of the T-55s and BM-21s – reaching Nabusanke between 7 and 9 March, nor about it receiving Amin's order to advance straight to Masaka and liberate the town, 'in three hours or less'. With this, they were less than 24km from the positions of the 201 Brigade JWTZ.Nyerere did not want to challenge Gaddafi, and actually sympathised with the PLO – although some elements of the latter were already involved in the fighting on the side of the UA. However, the JWTZ did not expect the Libyan appearance in the area between Nabusanke and Lukaya for a while longer. Therefore, emboldened by their earlier victories, the Tanzanians re-launched their advance on 10 March, expecting no special problems to be in their way.

Battle of Lukaya

As usual, the JWTZ attacked Lukaya from three sides: 207 Brigade

A Ugandan M4A1 Sherman tank, modified with HVSS suspension and wider (T80E5) tracks. It was armed with the M1A1C 76mm calibre gun and a M60 12.6mm calibre machine gun, and had two French-made smoke grenade dischargers installed on either side of the turret. Painted in bronze green, it carried rectangular identification markings in green and red on all four sides of the hull, and serial numbers (applied in white on black fields) on the front and rear hull. (Tom Cooper)

Originally delivered painted in olive green, Ugandan T-55As (all of Czechoslovak origin) were camouflaged through the addition of yellow or a sand colour applied in this unusually disruptive pattern. Except for turret numbers and the usual serials, they are not known to have worn any other kind of markings. (Tom Cooper)

A reconstruction of a Tanzanian Type-62 light tank from the late 1960s, when they still wore large turret designations. Exact details behind the system of these remains unknown. (Tom Cooper)

Nine Fouga CM.170 Magisters delivered from Israel in 1964 were the first jet trainers and combat aircraft of the UAAF. All were painted in colours that represented the contemporary standard of the Israeli Air Force, including brown (RAL 8008) and blue (RAL 5008) on the top surfaces and sides, and light grey (RAL 7044) on the under-surfaces. Except for having their noses marked with dayglo orange, they wore white serials in the range of U101–U109. (Tom Cooper)

A reconstruction of a Ugandan MiG-17F as seen in Entebbe in the late 1960s, when their camouflage consisted of brown (close to the RAL 8000, which tended to look like orange or dark tan in bright sunlight), blue (close to the RAL 5008) on the top surfaces, and either 'bare metal' or light grey (close to the RAL 7044) on the lower surfaces. (Tom Cooper)

A reconstruction of a Ugandan MiG-17F from the mid-1970s, by when most surviving aircraft of this type should have been repainted in grey (or, alternatively, in grey and sand on the top surfaces and sides). The U614 survived all subsequent wars and unrest, and is now posted as a second gate guard at Entebbe IAP. (Tom Cooper)

Probably the first MiG-21 delivered to Uganda was this MiG-21UM conversion trainer. Like the other two examples of this variant known to have been in service with the UAAF in the 1970s (serials U902 and U903), it arrived in 'bare metal'. Roundels were applied only in two positions (on the fin). (Tom Cooper)

While painted in 'air superiority grey', Ugandan MiG-21MFs had part of their rear fuselage not 'camouflaged', but painted in a dull aluminium colour, as was the practice on Nigerian and Somali examples. The example shown here (U907) is armed with a FAB-250M-54 bomb (250kg calibre) as was used for most air strikes in northern Tanzania. These were usually installed on inboard under-wing pylons, with the outboard pylons and centreline hardpoint being reserved for drop tanks. (Tom Cooper)

A reconstruction of one of several UAAF MiG-21MFs captured in a sabotaged condition at Entebbe on 10 April 1979. Contrary to contemporary assumptions based on poor photographs, they did not receive any kind of anti-glare panel in front of the cockpit, but this appeared to have been applied due to the removal of the avionics bay cover. U916 is shown armed with UB-16-57 pods for 16 S-5 57mm calibre unguided rockets. (Tom Cooper)

A reconstruction of a JWTZ F-6 from the late 1970s, before some of these aircraft received camouflage colours. As usual, large, four-digit serials were applied on the forward fuselage and the service title on the rear. National markings consisted of fin flashes only. (Tom Cooper)

A reconstruction of the camouflage pattern applied on at least some of the Tanzanian F-6s either during the war with Uganda in 1978–1979 or immediately afterwards. Of interest is the number of surfaces left in 'bare metal', and the Chinese variant of the ORO-57K rocket pod for six unguided 57mm calibre rockets, carried to enhance the armament consisting of three powerful NR-30 cannons installed internally. (Tom Cooper)

Despite intensive research over the years, many details about the markings of JWTZ MiG-21MFs remain uncertain. Painted in 'air superiority grey', they are certain to have received four-digit serials on the forward fuselage. However, whether the usual service title was applied as shown here, or if this was the case with national markings and serials on the fin, remains unclear. Their primary armament consisted of R-3S (AA-2 Atoll) air-to-air missiles and an internally-installed GSh-23 23mm calibre cannon. (Tom Cooper)

Most JWTZ DHC-4s received this camouflage pattern in grey and two shades of green during the Uganda-Tanzania War. This was necessary because of their frequent flights into the combat zone, during which they were hauling not only troop reinforcements, but often fuel and ammunition. Despite a high degree of satisfaction with the type, the Tanzanians had sold all of their DHC-4s by the end of 1979. (Tom Cooper)

The type that supplanted the DHC-4s in service during the war with Uganda was the DHC-5, an advanced variant with a navigational radar, more powerful engines and higher payload capacity. Four of these were in service in 1978 (two additional examples were delivered in 1981) and they arrived already camouflaged as shown here, in tan (FS30219), light green (FS34102) and dark green (FS34079) on the upper surfaces and sides, and light grey (FS36622) on the under-surfaces. (Tom Cooper)

Tanzania acquired three Hawker-Siddeley HS.748 Srs. 2A/314s between 1974 and 1978. Serialled JW9008, JW9009 and JW9010 (shown here), they provided faithful service during the war with Uganda. All three aircraft were camouflaged in light stone (BS361C/361, similar to the FS33717), dark green (BS381C/641, similar to the FS34079) and light grey (BS381C/637, similar to the FS35622). As was usually the case with Tanzanian transports, they had roundels applied in at least four positions and fin flashes; it is possible that their serials were repeated on the top surface of the right wing, and bottom surface of the left wing. (Tom Cooper)

A rare colour photograph of three Ugandan MiG-17Fs (and two C-47s) at the military side of Entebbe IAP in the late 1960s. All three have received the same camouflage pattern applied in colours similar to those used by the Israeli Air Force. (Albert Grandolini Collection)

All six of the C-47 Dakotas operated by the UAAF came from Israel and were thus already camouflaged in brown (the RAL 8008) and blue (the RAL 5008) on the top surfaces and sides, and light grey (the RAL 7044) on the under-surfaces, although these faded by the time this photograph was taken. Of interest is the application of roundels in six positions. (Albert Grandolini Collection)

Prior to the delivery of L-29s to Uganda, Czechoslovaks have painted these aircraft in a camouflage pattern similar to that applied on the UAAF's Magisters, but using their own colours including light grey (S-1110) and dark ochre (S-2210) on the upper surfaces and sides, and pastel grey (S-1010) on the under-surfaces. As can be seen here, serials were applied in black and national markings worn on six positions. (via Albert Grandolini)

Sometime during the early 1970s, some Ugandan L-29s were overhauled by Czechoslovaks and repainted – apparently in beige (BS381C/388) and an unknown shade of green on the upper surfaces and sides, and light admiralty grey (BS381C/627) on the under-surfaces. Note the L-29 with serial number U510 armed with a FAB-50 bomb (50kg calibre). (via Albert Grandolini)

A map of the major air bases, airfields and other known landing strips in Uganda. (Mark Lepko)

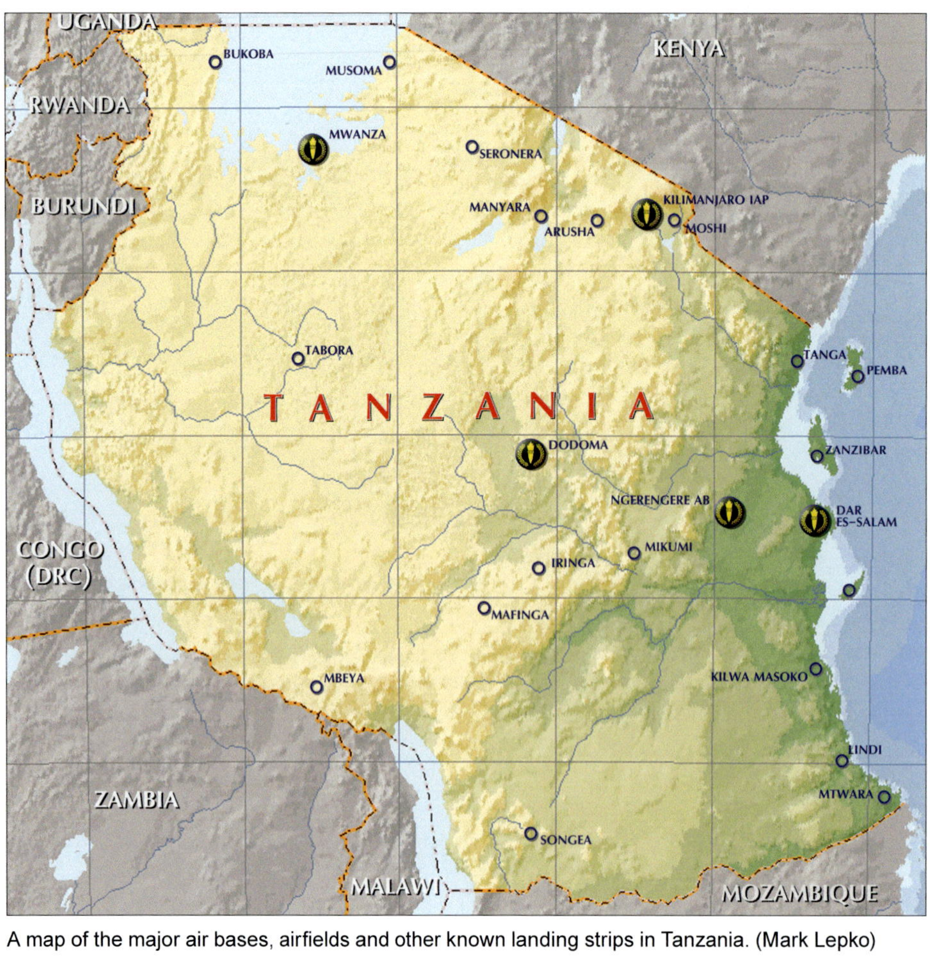

A map of the major air bases, airfields and other known landing strips in Tanzania. (Mark Lepko)

Civilians gather around an abandoned OT-64 APC of the Ugandan Army (registration number UA94). Of interest is the application of insignia in the form of a black diamond outlined in white on the front hull. The registration number ('UA94') was usually applied on the front and rear hull. (Mark Lepko Collection)

A close-up photograph of two Tanzanian MiG-21s from the famous 'MiG-row' at the military apron of Mwanza airfield. The nearest example appears to be a MiG-21UM with some sort of camouflage pattern, possibly consisting of green and dark brown over sand colours. In the centre is a MiG-21MF, painted blue-grey. JWTZ's MiG-21s should have scored their only aerial victory against Ugandan MiGs on 27 February 1979. (P. P. via Tom Cooper)

Tanzanian troops inspecting an abandoned Ugandan T-55A MBT. The UA crews have left six such tanks intact behind after the Battle of Simba Hills after offering only limited resistance. Note the very unusual disruptive camouflage pattern on this vehicle: it seems this was applied with the help of a big, round brush. (Albert Grandolini Collection)

advanced on the eastern flank, through the swamp; 208 Brigade on the western flank in a wide sweeping motion around and to the north of the swamp; and Brigadier Imran Kombe's 201 Brigade – an entirely new unit consisting of NPC-militia members – and a battalion of UPC troops under David Oyite Ojok assaulted down the road. Kisuule described what happened to his Artillery & Signals Regiment when the Tanzanians attacked:

Lukaya was still in our control but our soldiers had looted everything they could lay their hands on, and the locals had all fled. This made us a target anytime and for that reason I decided to put my tactical HQ in Buwama, at the county office, and I ordered all soldiers to stay 500m away from the centre. Unfortunately, they didn't follow orders and at around 1400 as I was setting up my base in Buwama, the Tanzanianas shot at us and eight of my soldiers were killed.

Eventually, 201 Brigade secured the town during the afternoon of 11 March and Kombe's forces began preparing to continue their advance along the causeway the next morning. All of a sudden Lukoya was then plastered by a barrage of BM-21 rockets. Moving down the causeway, the Libyans had spotted 201 Brigade and decided to attack before the Tanzanians could complete digging their trenches.

The rockets failed to cause any damage or casualties, but their loud screams and tails of flame as they passed low overhead scared the hell out of the inexperienced Tanzanian militiamen. Some broke and ran; others held out, but were then caught by advancing Libyan T-55 tanks (followed by three Ugandan M4A1 Shermans and a M38 Jeep) and their defences crumbled. Amazingly, not one JWTZ soldier was killed when the Libyans captured Lukaya: most managed to run into the swamps beside the road. However, although facing only three Tanzanian tanks further down the road, the LAA column then stopped. Kisuule continued:

The Libyans had now joined us and we positioned heavy guns they brought on the hills across Katonga. All of them facing Lukaya. We also deployed tanks. We planned to advance to Masaka on the next morning and briefed more than 1,000 Libyans at Mitala Maria … They came with many big guns that we did not have, like 122mm … After giving orders to both Libyans and Ugandan troops, at around 1500, I took valium and gave a tablet to Sule so that we [could] have enough sleep ahead of the long operation to retake Masaka. I was used to taking valium a day before any operation.

Msugiri and his commanders did not sleep but reacted quickly, issuing a series of orders. The three tanks south of the town were ordered to close the range and shell the enemy (when their crews showed some reluctance, more senior officers were sent to the scene to make sure the order was obeyed). 208 Brigade, meanwhile, nearly 60km (37 miles) north of Lukaya, was ordered to march back and cut the road between the Libyans and Kampala. Other officers began grouping volunteers from the disorganised ranks of 201 Brigade and sending them back to Lukaya to see what the enemy was doing. The night of 12 March was one of chaos and disorganisation on both sides, as Libyan, Palestinian, Ugandan Army, Tanzanian and Ugandan insurgent units intermingled in and outside the town in the darkness, repeatedly exchanging fire with friend and foe alike. Eight JWTZ troops and one of Ojok's men were killed in the process.[78]At dawn on 12 March, 208 Brigade reached the scene. Without taking any rest from its night-time race, it immediately launched a counter-attack, hitting the Libyans from the front and then from the back. Terrific amounts of very precise artillery and rocket fire tore into the Libyan positions, causing such shock and heavy casualties that neither LAA troops nor the Ugandans accompanying them managed to fire back. Kisuule described the catastrophe that befell the Artillery & Signals Regiment and allied Libyans as follows:

We were woken up by the stampede of the fleeing Libyans [–] their Jeeps which had been facing Lukaya were now retreating to Kampala. I told Major Aloysius Ndibowa to blow the road so they don't retreat … The fighting was so fierce and many of my men were killed and tens of Jeeps were ferrying dead bodies from the front line to Kampala. The Saba-Saba rocket launchers were giving us a real hard time.

After the Battle of Lukaya, the Ugandan Army de-facto collapsed and ran. Tanzanian infantry are shown with a group of Ugandan troops, some of whom have already changed into civilian clothing. (Albert Grandolini Collection)

The direction, speed and ferocity of 208 Brigade's attack were such that whoever could, broke and ran – only to find that the crack Tanzanian crack unit had blocked the causeway towards the north, as concluded by Kisuule:

Immediately after Katonga Bridge … there was an [sic] eucalyptus forest on the side of the road. There the Tanzanians had laid a death trap for us. Many of our infantrymen, including Libyans, were killed there. Sule, who had been walking behind the tanks, was crushed by one of the tanks as it tried to reverse in retreat … That day we lost many soldiers … Unfortunately, there was laxity on our side: had we kept the momentum, we would have taken back Masaka.

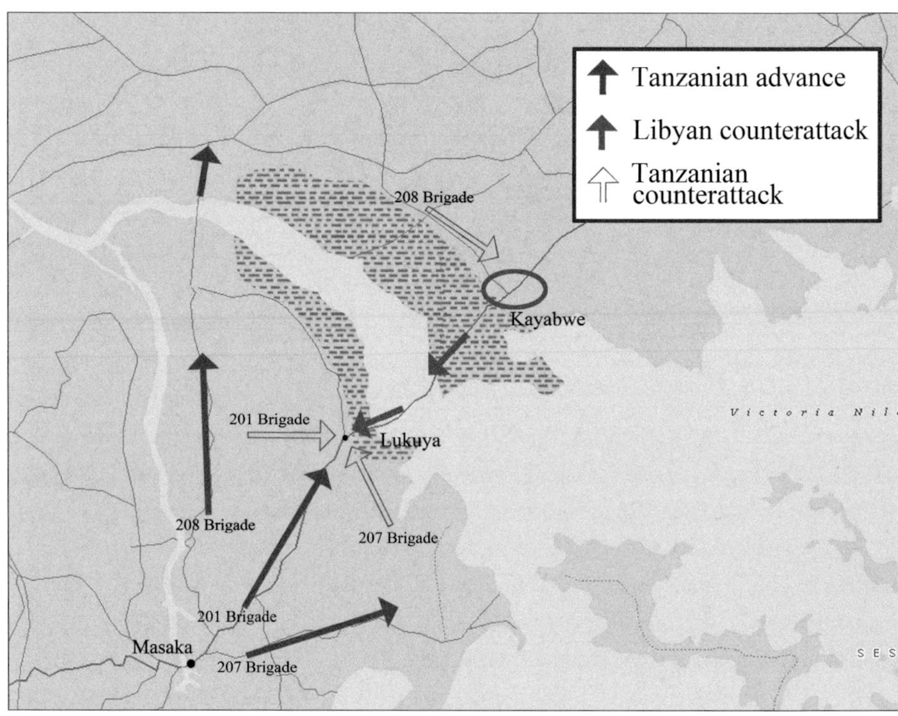

A map showing all three phases of the Battle of Lukaya, fought on 10 and 11 March 1979. Three JWTZ brigades approached the area, with 208 Brigade advancing on the left flank in a northerly direction, 201 Brigade taking Lukaya in the centre and 207 Brigade securing the eastern flank. The 201 Brigade secured Lukaya but was then hit by a sudden Libyan-Ugandan counter-attack and thrown back. Finally, 208 Brigade counter-attacked into the northern flank and the back of the Libyan-Ugandan group of forces, while the 201 and 207 recovered Lukaya. (Tom Cooper)

Libyans and Ugandans were finished when the regrouped 201 attacked their main positions from the south, closing the trap. When the shooting stopped, the bodies of over 200 LAA and 200 UA soldiers littered the battlefield.[79]

Tigers at Sembabule

At the same time that they faced a major crisis at Lukaya, the Tanzanians found themselves in even bigger trouble in western Uganda. Namely, while advancing from Masaka to Kampala and from Mbarara towards the north-west, the JWTZ failed to take into account the main base of the Tiger Regiment UA in Mubende, halfway between the two major groups of the Tanzanian army. Admittedly, 205 Brigade was sent from Masaka to intercept the Ugandan unit, but this brand new formation lacked experience in hill combat and was taken by surprise when it ran into elements of the Tiger Regiment entrenched at Sembabule, about 60km (37 miles) north-west of Masaka. After recovering from the initial shock, the Tanzanians regrouped and attacked again, capturing some Ugandan positions – only to see these retaken the next day by Amin's forces. Time and again, they would find corpses of their comrades, decapitated, with the severed head placed on the chest: this dispirited the young Tanzanian militiamen, causing entire companies and then battalions to flee when fired upon. After two weeks of largely fruitless attacks and the loss of about 20 troops, Major-Genaral Myunga decided to reorganise 205 Brigade. Brig Lupogo was replaced by Brig Muhiddin Kirmario – a soldier-politician (an elected member of parliament and regional

Idi Amin inspecting Libyan Army troops on their arrival at Entebbe IAP. (Albert Grandolini Collection)

A Libyan Tu-22 bomber of the same type as at least two which were deployed to Nakasangola AB, in northern Uganda, sometime in early March 1979. They flew a number of air strikes against locations in Tanzania, and even in Uganda, but all of their bombs missed their targets by a wide margin. (AMI via David Cenciotti)

commander in Mwanza) – who immediately went to meet his officers and soldiers. Kirmario promised his troops to march into the battle with them, abandoned the small-unit tactics and instead employed 'advance to contact' tactics, moving the entire brigade as a single entity until the enemy was engaged and overpowered. Kirmario's methods worked: with new spirit instilled in them, the troops of the 205 breached the positions of the Tiger Regiment, causing it a loss of 25 KIA in the process and forcing survivors to flee.[80] Even then, the Tanzanians secured Sembabule only on 5 April.Further west, another part of the Tiger Regiment delivered a particularly effective counter-attack on the 80th Battalion (CO Major Mosha), which was advancing in the direction of Ntungamo, on 21 March. Although supported by three tanks, the Tanzanian infantry fell back and it took a counter-attack of the Special Forces Battalion of 206 Brigade (CO Major Kessy) into the Ugandan left flank to stabilise the situation. The UA unit then fell back into Ntungamo. Similarly, when the 2nd Battalion of 206 Brigade approached Fort Portal – an important town close to the border with Zaire – it collided with remnants of the Mountains of the Moon Battalion and was partially dispersed.[81]

Interrupted Advance on Kampala

The catastrophe at Lukaya did not prevent the Libyan government from continuing to deploy additional troops and supplies to Uganda. Every night, Tanzanian radar at Mwanza tracked a number of aircraft which landed in Entebbe to unload fresh troops and supplies and then evacuate injured back to Tripoli.[82] However, much of the equipment brought in piled up around the airport because the Libyans and Ugandans were much too disorganised to arrange its distribution. Despite Libyan reinforcements, chaos and panic spread among Ugandan troops scattered along the road to Kampala, causing a near-collapse of the military, as recalled by Kisuule:

> *Many of the commanders who had survived up to Nyendo instead retreated back to Kampala. When I got backto Buwama, I found Major-Genaral Gowan had also left, [and] all the commanders had deserted the front. I told the remaining forces to withdraw back to Buwama. Once there, I found out that the withdrawing troops were wreaking havoc in Masindi, looting everything they could.*

Unsurprisingly, the Tanzanians launched a swift advance towards the Ugandan capital. 207 and 208 Brigades captured Mpigi, while the 201 swept wide to the west to intersect the road and railway connecting Kampala to Fort Portal. Elements of the latter brigade came across a Libyan unit encamped near Mityana and killed 30 in a quick attack. The only other resistance the JWTZ experienced during the last few days of March was caused by mud from ceaseless rain.With their ground forces confused and fleeing, but still attempting to force Dar es-Salaam to call off its invasion, Gaddafi issued an explicit threat to Nyerere, demanding that he withdraw Tanzanian troops within 24 hours or face a full-scale Libyan involvement on Amin's side. Although taken aback, Nyerere ordered his commanders to continue. The Libyans and Ugandans then launched a number of air strikes on Tanzania. Late on 1 April, a LAAF Tu-22 bomber which approached at low altitude over Lake Victoria attempted to hit the fuel depot at Mwanza. The bombs missed not only all of their targets but the entire city, and landed in a nearby game reserve, injuring one person and killing six antelope and several birds.[83] Similarly, another attack by Tu-22s against one of the Tanzanian bases south of the border ended with Libyan bombs landing near Nyarubanga – inside Burundi![84] In response to the attacks by Libyan bombers, the Air Wing JWTZ hit back in force, hitting fuel depots in Kampala, Jinja and Tororo, all of which were set on fire. One of the bombs flattened the building of the Libya-Uganda Development Bank in Jinja and caused Amin – who was in the town during this attack – to run into the street screaming incoherently.[85]An attack on Entebbe IAP, two days later, was less effective. Although the terminal was set ablaze by a number of hits by 57mm rockets, the runway remained intact, enabling Libyan transports to continue using it. Monitoring the Entebbe Peninsula from the hills near Mpigi, JWTZ commanders concluded that – contrary to their original plan to advance straight for Kampala – they would first have to destroy the Libyan and Ugandan troops concentrated around Entebbe IAP, before continuing to the Ugandan capital.The Tanzanian assault began during the evening of 6 April with a massive artillery barrage. This covered the movement of 208 Brigade, which moved in, setting up ambushes on all roads in the area. Around 1000 the next morning, JWTZ toops were about the reach the airport when a Libyan C-130 landed

During their advance on Kampala – and even more so afterwards – the Tanzanian military began making extensive use of confiscated civilian trucks to transport its infantry. This Mercedes-Benz is somewhere in the suburbs of the Ugandan capital. (Albert Grandolini Collection)

A still from a video showing the smouldering wreckage of LAAF C-130H serial number 116, shot down on take-off from Entebbe IAP by a Tanzanian RPG-7 on 6 April 1979. (Pit Weinter Collection)

Ugandan civilians cheering a Tanzanian Type-59 MBT rolling through the suburbs of Kampala on 7 April 1979. Notable is the heavy camouflage pattern applied on this vehicle – apparently in yellow or sand colour applied crudely over the original olive green. Also of interest is the heavy foliage attached by the crew to their tank. (Albert Grandolini Collection)

Tanzanian troops inspecting the wreckage of UAAF aircraft at Entebbe in mid-April 1979. Behind them is the MiG-21MF serial number U618 or U619, but also several wooden cases with 250kg calibre bombs. The fact that the ejection seat appears to have been fired out of the cockpit and the avionics bay in front of the cockpit was ripped open, points at sabotage by withdrawing Ugandan personnel. (Pit Weinert Collection)

to pick up as many troops trapped there as possible. While taxi-ing for take-off, the Hercules was hit by a RPG-7-grenade fired by one of the Tanzanian advance parties and set on fire, incarcerating everybody inside. With the noose rapidly tightening around them, the remaining Libyans made a break for the capital in a long convoy consisting of several large trucks and two armoured cars. After travelling for 8km, the column ran into an ambush set up by 208 Brigade. Remaining motionless and silent, Tanzanian troops waited patiently as the convoy approached before coming to a halt: they could see Libyan commanders conferring for a while before one of the armoured cars sprayed the side of the road with machine-gun fire. Unaffected, they held their fire and let both armoured cars through without incident. However, when the trucks entered the gap, Colonel Boma gave the order to attack, unleashing 400 troops downhill upon the shocked enemy: both armoured cares were knocked out by RPGs, and within ten minutes 65 Libyans were killed.[86]Overall, more than 300 Libyan troops were killed in and around Entebbe and 59 taken POW (10 of these were not even Libyan citizens) on 7 and 8 April. Dozens were evacuated to Mulago Hospital in Kampala, then to Nakasangola AB and flown back to their homeland. Gaddafi's adventure in Uganda was about to end in an unmitigated disaster.Also captured at Entebbe were about 200 officers and airmen of the UAAF, 12 more or less non-operational and damaged MiGs and a burned-out hulk of a Uganda Airlines Boeing 707. Most other UAAF personnel fled to Jinja and Nakasangola, spreading panic and defecting along the way. This left the last C-in-C UAAF, Lieutenant-Colonel Andrew Mukooza (former CO of the MiG-17 Squadron) without aircraft and crews to continue the fight. Elsewhere, after refusing the order to move south and launch a counter-attack, elements of the UA in Soroti, in the north of the country, mutinied against the government and established themselves in control. Similarly, the last UA units in Tororo mutinied and sided with Ugandan exile insurgents, helping them secure the town.[87]

Fall of Idi Amin

The fall of Entebbe not only ended the Libyan airlift effort, but resulted in the final collapse of the entire Ugandan military. Although their units were not yet ready for a major assault, and their MiGs were still busy attempting to hit one of the major ammunition depots in the city, the Tanzanians decided to rush advance parties around and into the Ugandan capital, but to leave open the road to Jinja as the last avenue of escape for surviving Libyans and diplomats in the city. 208 Brigade was to attack from the south, the 207 and one UNLA battalion from the west, while the 201 was to block all exits from Kamapla towards the north. The major role

Not all of the Tanzanians had to march all the way from Kampala to Jinja: the JWTZ took great care to use whatever suitable vehicles it could get and rotate these to transport elements of all three brigades involved in the advance. This truck full of Tanzanian troops is in Kampala on 19 April 1979. (Albert Grandolini Collection)

A bloody scene of the last battle between Amin's troops and Tanzanian forces near Lira, in early May 1979. It shows the column of UA Land Rovers and truck-towed artillery pieces knocked out by mortars of 201 Brigade JWTZ. (Albert Grandolini Collection)

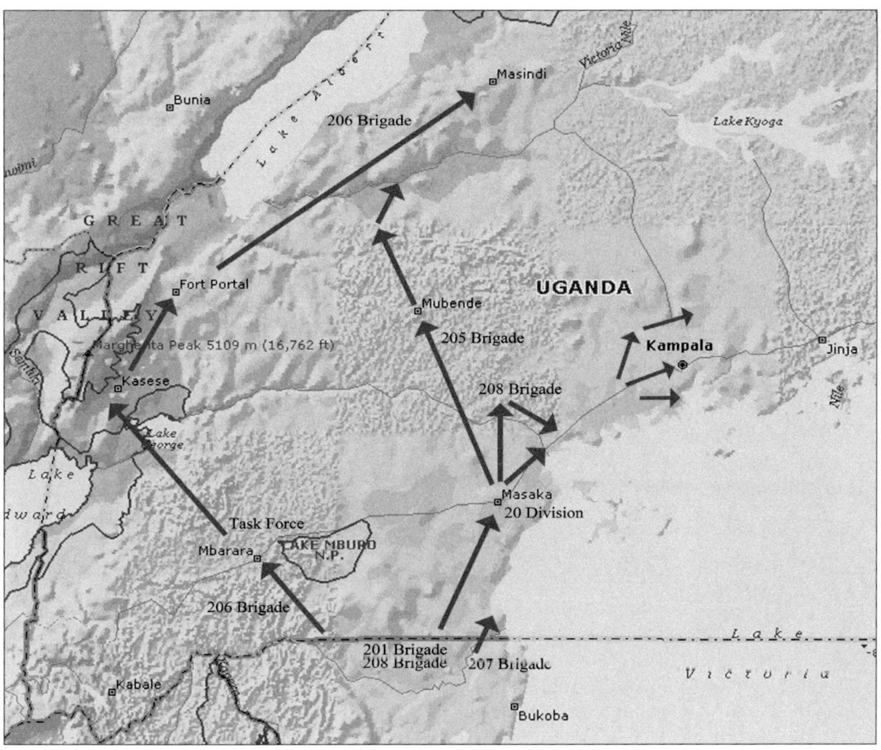

A map of the Tanzanian invasion of Uganda, from February–May 1979. (Tom Cooper)

in this operation was played by the 800-strong 19th Battalion (CO Colonel Ben Msuya) of 208 Brigade – a unit that had not lost a single soldier since the start of the war.[88]Tanzanians entered Kampala from three sides on 10 April in the face of chaotic and sporadic resistance, although not without the 19th Battalion suffering its only two losses of the conflict in a skirmish with a Ugandan T-55 tank. The 'escape hatch' for Libyans proved effective in so far as it enabled survivors to fade from the battlefield without the disgrace of ending in Tanzanian captivity. However, it also allowed Idi Amin and his top officials to get away, most of them fleeing to Libya, Sudan or Zaire.After a week and a half in Kampala, JWTZ units continued their advance towards Jinja and the nearby Owen Falls hydroelectric station. Once again, the proud 208 Brigade was in the lead but, contrary to previous times, this time the Tanzanians made extensive use of buses and trucks. Although there was never enough transportation, this at least meant that not all the troops had to march there. Despite Amin's promises to make his last stand in the town, and although a few hundred soldiers could have easily defended the position, Jinja was actually defended by only 19 scared stragglers. The 3,000 troops of the 208 assaulted Jinja as soon as reconnaissance reported no defences on the eastern bank of the Victoria Nile: one battalion secured the near side of the bridge and the structure itself, a second battalion sprinted across and secured the east bank and a third battalion then moved across the secured bridge in the direction of the Eagle Colonel Gaddafi Barracks, where 12 abandoned MBTs and APCs, plus a huge stock of ammunition, were captured.With this, the war in Uganda was effectively over, even though some Tanzanian units still had to complete their advances into other parts of northern and north-western Uganda. By the end of April, the JWTZ had also taken Nakasangola AB and Gulu airfield, where the last remaining UAAF MiG-17s and L-29s were captured. The final major action of the war was fought outside Lira, on the border with Sudan,

Tanzanian troops at the Owen Dam, outside Jinja, in late April 1979. (Albert Grandolini Collection)

Tanzanian troops at rest in Kampala in mid-April 1979. Characteristically for those chaotic days, one of them has got himself a transistor-radio – a much sought-after booty. (Albert Grandolini Collection)

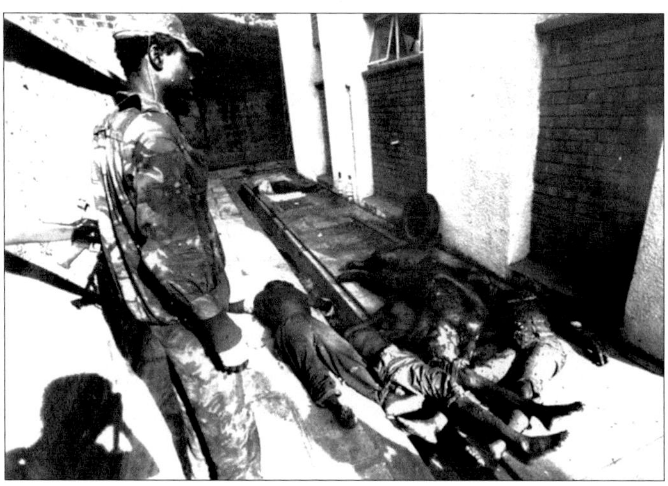

A tragic scene from the notorious compound of the SRB-HQ, where Tanzanian troops found dozens of bodies of victims of Amin's rule of terror. (Albert Grandolini Collection)

For most of their advance into downtown Kampala, troops of the 19th Battalion/208 Brigade JWTZ were more troubled by the masses of cheering civilians than with resistance from the Ugandan Army. (Albert Grandolini Collection)

Troops and one of the Type-62 light tanks of 208 Brigade JWTZ during the advance on Jinja, the second largest city in Uganda, on 18 April 1979. (Albert Grandolini Collection)

After completing the rather easy task of conquering Kampala, Tanzanian troops continued their slow advance into northern Uganda. The machine-gunner of this Type-62 light tank cheerfully played the accordion during the march on Gulu in late April 1979. (Albert Grandolini Collection)

Two crew members of a JWTZ tank with colleagues in a Land Rover carrying a 'Dushka' 12.7mm calibre machine gun. Towards the end of the war, most Tanzanian tanks were in bad shape after the long advance across Uganda. Nearly all had trouble with worn-out batteries, replacements for which failed to reach the front on time. During the advance on Moroto, for example, only one of three JWTZ Type 59s was able to start itself and had to tow the other two to get them started. When even that tank failed, all three had to be left behind. (Albert Grandolini Collection)

in early May. There the advance elements of 201 Brigade JWTZ encountered a column of UA Land Rovers mounting recoilless rifles, supported by two anti-aircraft guns. The seasoned veterans of the 201 remained calm this time: although hopelessly outranged, they quickly understood that the enemy gunners were not only using the wrong type of ammunition, but were also poor aimers. The Tanzanians therefore continued advancing under fire until their mortars were within range: the Ugandan column was then hit with murderous precision and most vehicles and their occupants were destroyed in a matter of minutes.The war thus ended in total defeat for Uganda, which remained under Tanzanian occupation until 1982. As far as is known, Tanzania lost 373 soldiers, of whom 96 were killed by enemy fire: the rest died in accidents. The UNLA had lost about 150, most of them in the Lake Victoria boat sinking. There is no way to precisely asses the number of Ugandan and Libyan casualties, but most reasonable estimates cite about 600 as Gaddafi's and 1,000 as Amin's causalties. Last, but not least, Tanzania also lost around 1,500 civilians in the Kagera Salient and about 500 Ugandan civilians were killed – accidentally or intentionally – by both sides during the war.[89]

CHAPTER FOUR:
FROM ONE WAR INTO ANOTHER

In late March 1979, while the JWTZ was still advancing on Kampala, representatives of all the Ugandan opposition movements met in Moshi. There they agreed to regroup all of their respective armed units within the UNLA. A shadow government led by Yusufu Lule – a seasoned politician – was set up as centrepiece of a new authority, the Uganda National Liberation Front (UNLF), on 13 April, just two days after Tanzanians captured Kampala. Although everybody knew that Lule's government was 'provisional' by nature and all political parties agreed to organise new elections within two years, rivalries and internal struggle ripped the new government apart before long. Lule was dismissed on 20 June and replaced by Godfrey Binaisa, an outsider without a wide support base. In turn, Binaisa was demoted by the Military Commission of the UNLF in May 1980.The Military Commission of the UNLF – which was an ad-hoc body – originally took over intending to rule the country until elections which were scheduled for December 1980. Its provisional Minister of Defence was Yoweri Museveni, who now found himself fighting a lost political battle against his two closest subordinates – Major-General Tito Okello and Brig David Oyite Ojok – being close associates of Milton Obote, and in a far better position to maintain their dominance over new institutions. Disappointed, Museveni founded the Uganda Patriotic Movement (UPM) in mid-1980, intending to run against the DP, the Conservative Party and Obote's UPC. However, Obote proved much more experienced and better organised: his party won the elections, obtaining 72 out of 126 seats in the parliament, followed by the DP with 51 seats. The UPM won only one seat. Museveni contested the elections, denouncing them as heavily rigged – and was soon proven right, at least indirectly, when Obote was inaugurated President of Uganda for the second time and launched a wave of repression against all opposition groups.[90]Other parties heavily contested the UPC too, but while the DP opted for legal opposition, most of the other movements – foremost among them the Uganda Army (UA, Amin loyalists), the Uganda Freedom Fighters (UFF, led by Yusufe Lule) and the conservative Uganda Freedom Movement (UFM) – decided to launch an insurgency. Thus began the next armed conflict in Uganda, also known as the 'Bush War'.[91]

West Nile

Usually known as the West Front (WF) or Western Nile Front, the Uganda Army was one of the first insurgent movements to become active inside Uganda in 1980. Grouped around a number of ex-UA officers who took refugee in Sudan and Zaire, and led by Major-Genaral Bernard Lumago, it recruited heavily through Idi Amin's power-base and eventually assembled a force of about 7,100, including 100 officers, 5,500 former soldiers, and 1,500 new volunteers.[92] Organised into battalions of around 400 each, although only about 50 percent of available officers and other ranks were armed, the WF began launching serious operations during the autumn of 1980. On 6 October it overran the town of Koboko and killed the CO of the local UNLA garrison. Two days later, it took the UNLA garrison in Bondo by surprise and slaughtered most of the troops during the morning parade; and on 9 October, insurgents captured the town of Arua and the local airport. Not intending to expose themselves to the full might of the rebuilt UNLA, the WF subsequently withdrew into Sudan.After reorganising and replenishing, the Ugandan Army group launched its second major foray into Uganda shortly before the general elections in December 1980. As one of the opening moves, its insurgents ambushed a convoy carrying Milton Obote while it was touring the region during the election campaign: the lead vehicle was destroyed and all occupants killed, but the other two – including the car carrying Tito Okello – managed to escape.[93] Subsequently, the WF overran Koboko again and established its own provisional administration, progressively gaining control over most of the West Nile Province – although UNLA garrisons remained in control of major towns. Subsequently, this insurgent group proved vulnerable to internal power struggles: during the same month, the WF split into the Uganda National Rescue Front (UNRF) and the Former Uganda National Army (FUNA). The leader of the latter – British- and Israeli-trained Brig Moses Ali – was eager to disassociate himself from the cumbersome heritage of Idi Amin's rule. On the contrary, FUNA's leadership became involved in smuggling operations. The rivalry between these two movements degenerated into an armed conflict in which Ali's troops gained the upper hand. However, the actual victor was the UNLA, which destroyed most of the UNRF during the Christmas offensive in December 1982, and subsequently ran an operation of large-scale looting and massacres, driving over 260,000 refugees into Sudan and Zaire and ruining the insurgent infrastructure.[94]

Ordeal of the UFM

The UFM experienced a very similar fate. Founded in 1980 by Balaki Kirya, a respected political figure who lived in exile in Nairobi, and largely staffed by disgruntled soldiers, the UFM's operations inside Uganda were led by Dr Andrew Kayira, a criminologist by profession.[95] While its fighters were considered well-disciplined (within a Ugandan context), the aim of this organisation – toppling Obote's government by straightforward attacks – was what doomed it to fail from the beginning. The UFM was also flawed because of internecine rivalries within its leadership and because it never implemented any uniformed recruitment or training procedures. While anyone was welcome to enlist, this also meant that the whole group was vulnerable to infiltration by enemy intelligence operatives.The first major operation of the UFM was a general attack on Kampala, launched on 9 February 1981, targeting symbolic places such as the Post Office or the Radio Uganda Building. Although taking the UNLA by surprise and striking a psychological blow, the insurgents failed to cause a collapse of the government.Another large-scale attack on Kampala followed on 23 February 1982, with the HQ of the UNLA Central Brigade at the Lubiri Hill being the primary target. However, the 300 involved fighters failed to penetrate the base because their aim was very poor. The Army then launched a fierce pursuit operation in the course of which most of the insurgents' weapons were lost. Furthermore, the UFM then failed to expolit the fact that the government launched a three-day wave of ferocious reprisals against the city's Baganda population, which was summarily considered as accomplices of the attackers.[96] The over-confident UFM then made another mistake by trying to regroup its fighters within one of the zones under the control of Museveni's group: although its leaders managed to convince a few insurgents from the latter to defect and join them, one of the UFM's offiers defected too – and delivered a stock of more than 200 rifles with him.[97]While Kayira was forced to flee into exile in September 1982, his followers regrouped and launched an attack on Kitala prison. How poorely prepared this operation was became obvious when it turned out that the facility was protected by a well-entrenched platoon of UNLA troops.The final nails in the UFM's coffin were delivered in 1983. First of all, Obote's intelligence identified all the main insurgent camps, his forces attacked them and inflicted serious losses on the guerrillas. In July 1983, Kirya was kidnapped in Nairobi and repatriated to Uganda, where he was jailed. Afterwards, the UFM was essentially a spent force that never reached any semblance of importance.

Museveni's Struggle for Survival

Museveni and his associates of the former FRONASA saw an armed struggle as the only option left to remove Obote's government. However, they were initially facing great odds, because of Museveni's inability to establish himself in control of the MOD. Their opponents used every trick in the book – including insufficient height – to prevent enlistment of FRONASA fighters into the UNLA: the 4,000 (out of about 9,000 combatants Museveni controlled by mid-1979) who were accepted were dispersed over most different units around the country, well away from the capital. Furthermore, the FRONASA had to give away all of its weapons and supplies while being integrated into the Ugandan National Liberation Army. Concluding that an armed coup against Obote was de-facto impossible – also because of the presence of Tanzanian troops – Museveni opted for launching a protracted guerrilla war, following the Maoist pattern of a 'people's war'. He began rallying his small core of trusted followers, initially consisting of his own bodyguards and a few ex-FRONASA officers still present in the Kampala area. This small group proved vital not only for Museveni's survival during the first few months of their armed struggle, but eventually formed the core of what became the Popular Resistance Army (PRA).

Museveni next began re-establishing ties with numerous sympathisers in Kampala and elsewhere around Uganda. Some of these ran underground networks which proved capable of providing logistical and financial support, but also recruiting and transferring new recruits to different guerrilla sanctuaries. These networks were to prove crucial in allowing a number of trained and combat-experienced officers and other ranks of the UNLA – like Lieutenant Pecos Kutesa – to join the Popular Resistance Army. The efforts of the PRA were made easier by most Ugandans considering Obote and his government as 'northerners in essence'. Although Obote's security services were – apparently – aware of Museveni's activities, they hesitated to remove him because the Tanzanians were still hoping Museveni might join the new government.[98]

Through 1980, the clock was ticking very fast for the PRA: while waiting for a shipment of weapons from abroad that never materialised, the group had several of its potential ex-FRONASA officers assassinated by Obote's followers. With little other option, the group began planning an attack against the Kabamba training camp. This objective was selected with the aim of seizing much-needed weapons and ammunition, but also striking a resounding propaganda blow to mark the beginning of its armed struggle against the new government.[99] Another reason was that although garrisoning the JWTZ troops, the Kabamba camp was a primary recruiting centre, which meant that the PRA was capable of infiltrating several sympathisers who provided very detailed intelligence. Also, the main arms depot of this facility was located near its main entrance, which meant that the assailants could – provided they operated fast enough – hope to plunder this without having to fight down and defeat the entire garrison.[100]

The attack on Kabamba was launched during the evening of

Tanzanian President Nyerere (centre, with a shield) during victory celebrations after the war with Uganda. Recognising that the Ugandan population was unlikely to appreciate any lasting presence of foreign troops, and troubled by the financial strain of JWTZ's deployment in Uganda, he was quick to withdraw Tanzanian troops from the country at the first opportunity. (Albert Grandolini Collection)

Partly because Tanzanians took away much of the captured heavy equipment (including most of the UAAF's MiG-21s which were still intact), the UNLA was left with very little to start with. Among others, it returned four M4 Shermans to working condition, but at least one of these was abandoned during the fighting with the NRA in the early 1980s. (Albert Grandolini Collection)

6 February 1981, when a group of 34 fighters (armed with only 27 firearms) led by Museveni left Kampala in two vehicles. They reached their objective early the next morning, only to find that their plan was compromised when one of the sentries at the main gate managed to open fire before he was killed. Alerted by the gunshots, another of the UNLA troops managed to entrench himself inside the armoury and thus deny the group access to this vital source of arms and ammunition. Undaunted, Museveni and his followers attacked and captured six vehicles and a few guns before deciding to withdraw, while suffering only one casualty: a fighter who was shot in the leg.[101]

After this first, partial failure, the PRA ran a number of attacks on police stations, capturing additional firearms in the process – including a single RPG-7 launcher. However, on 9 February, the group came under attack from JWTZ and UNLA units near the town of Kiboga and was forced to scatter. About a week later, the PRA reunited and – with exception of about a dozen men who decided to give up the armed struggle – ambushed a Tanzanian military vehicle on 18 February. At this stage, Museveni and his followers were lacking secure bases to retreat to; they could not even light fires to cook or build huts in order to avoid detection. Without extensive aid provided by their supporters within the local population, they would certainly prove unable to continue their armed struggle.[102]

UNLA in Trouble

The crucial reason why the PRA and then the NRA survived this early period of insurgency – while still extremely vulnerable – was that the UNLA was simultaneously facing many different threats around the country. Reacting to multiple and rather distant threats was no easy task for the UNLA: not only was this force new and lacking experience in counter-insurgency (COIN) warfare, but the new Ugandan military was weakened by rivalries between former Kikosi Maalum and other ex-FRONASA officers. Although the new UNLA grew in size from 7,346 men in November 1979 to more than 15,000 by December 1981, most of these were scattered all over the country.[103] Furthermore, the majority of new recruits came from the Acholi and Lango ethnic groups, and the military thus quickly began to be perceived as an alien force by a majority of Ugandans.

On the other hand, although the defence budget took away up to 23 percent of the government expenditures in 1981–1982, most of spending was invested in security services responsible for maintaining Obote in power.[104] This resulted in the majority of UNLA troops remaining permanently underpaid, prompting many officers into corruption. Unsurprisingly, most government units soon gained a reputation for looting and lack of discipline – which, although successful against the WF and UFM in the short term, was to prove disastrous in the course of the COIN campaign against the far more sophisticated PRA.[105]

Another major problem which plagued the UNLA was a significant difference in tactical effectiveness of its different units, which was a direct result of their training by a host of foreign advisers. For example, the Central Brigade (CO Brig Gen Bazilio Olara Okello), which bore the brunt of fighting against the NRA during the first year of the insurgency, was hopelessly inferior in comparison to units which fought the UNRF in northern Uganda. Largely consisting of barely-trained militiamen known as 'Not-Yet-Allocated Army Numbers' (NYA), it was considered 'cannon fodder' even by its commanders. Indeed, if it was not for Tanzanian support, much of the UNLA would have collapsed by the end of 1981.[106]At least as troublesome was the sorry state of the Ugandan economy. After years of corruption and mismanagement under Amin, Obote proved almost as inept a ruler. Despite his formerly leftist political viewpoints, he obtained international funding by willingly applying the structural adjustment programmes recognised by the International Monetary Fund. While the resulting policies had some positive effect in decreasing inflation and prompting slow economic recovery, Uganda remained plagued by endemic corruption, neglected infrastructure and massive investment into the UNLA.

Tanzanian Withdrawal

The influence of the JWTZ was paramount during the formative years of the new Ugandan military.As early as August 1979, the first contingent of 300 Ugandan cadets – largely officers purged during Amin's rule – was sent for a 10-month course at the Tanzanian National Leadership Academy in Monduli.[107] Numerous instructors from Tanzania – but also from North Korea and Ethiopia – helped train military ranks at various locations around Uganda, and operational UNLA units were supported by a 10,000-strong contingent of JWTZ troops and 1,000 Tanzanian policemen who remained in the country. However, lack of money to maintain such a massive presence forced Nyerere to withdraw his troops: the last of them left Uganda in June 1981, leaving behind between 800 and 1,000 advisers.[108]The Tanzanian withdrawal put the UNLA under additional pressure. Obote's government then managed to obtain only minimal support from other countries and thus proved unable to significantly bolster its fledgling armed forces. For example, a British private military company (PMC) Falconstar Ltd. trained about 1,500 troops of Special Forces (a new unit nominally attached to the Police, wearing distinctive brick red and yellow uniforms) between 1981 and 1983.[109] A Commonwealth Military Training Team of 36 instructors from seven countries (including the UK and Australia) arrived in 1982. North Korea began providing 14.5mm and 12.7mm calibre machine guns and 107mm calibre multiple rocket launchers with 12 tubes, and a team of its advisers trained Ugandan troops in their use in late 1982, sometimes 'accompanying' their students to the front lines.[110]

Because the once-powerful UAAF was completely destroyed during the Tanzanian invasion, the UNLA lacked any kind of air support. The MOD attempted to rebuild an air wing, starting in 1980, but lack of funding compelled it to limit its ambitions to the establishment of a small helicopter squadron equipped with few Agusta-Bell AB.205 and AB.206 helicopters which had been acquired from Libya during Amin's rule. More intensive operations of these were prevented by Washington, which refused to sell military versions of the helicopters; instead, the Ugandans were advised to request help from Agusta-Bell in Italy. In 1985, Kampala placed an order for six AB.412SPs in Rome, but these were delivered only when it was much too late for them to be a factor. Meanwhile, Uganda contracted J & S Franklin Ltd in London, using a Canadian front company, to buy three Bell 206Bs and three Bell 214s built for the Bahamas directly from the USA, but which were never paid for by Nassau. The Canadian front company rushed to pay for these helicopters and they were delivered in 1982, arriving together with three civilian experts – including a Swiss engineer and two Canadians (one a pilot and other a mechanic) – who were to serve as instructors for Ugandan pilots. Although UNLA officers suspected the three well-paid expatriates to be much less experienced than promised, they did help establish the Helicopter Squadron. This unit, led by Captain Peter Oringi, eventually proved its value by flying reconnaissance, liaison, casualty-evacuation and resupply missions.[111]

Popular to National Resistance Army

Meanwhile, Museveni's PRA was well on the way to recovery. Following several weeks of getting rest and some food, and after another expected arms shipment failed to materialise, the insurgents launched their next operation on 18 March, when they ambushed several UNLA vehicles outside Kawanda. On 5 April, a more ambitious enterprise took place when Museveni attacked the UNLA's outpost in Kakiri: organised into five sections (for details of the PRA's contemporary 'order of battle', see Table 9), 50 fighters attacked this small garrison after a night march and swiftly overran it, capturing one machine gun, two 60mm mortars and 12 sub-machine guns, together with ammunition. While withdrawing from the site, insurgents also killed a Tanzanian major who arrived with a JWTZ truck. Subsequently, the PRA hastily retreated into the nearby forest, randomly mortared by Tanzanians supported by at least one APC.[112]

Table 9: Organisation of the PRA, late March/early April 1981[113]

Unit	Commander
1st Section	Yoweri Museveni
2nd Section	Sam Magara
3rd Section	Jack Muchunguzi
4th Section	Hannington Mugabi
5th Section	Fred Rwigyema

A few days later, the PRA split into two groups: one, led by Sam Magara, deployed along the Kampala–Bombo road; the other, led by Elly Tumwine, took positions along the Kampala–Hoima road.[114] However, Tumwine's group was tracked down by a company of JWTZ infantry and attacked at dawn on 18 April. One insurgent was KIA during the short fire-fight and the others forced to scatter, losing some of the weapons captured at Kakiri.[115] Survivors re-united with Rwigyema's group several days later, and then concentrated on recruiting and training new fighters, until the PRA counted about 200 men in late April and early May.[116]In June, Museveni travelled to Nairobi in Kenya to meet Yusuf Lule, leader of the UFF. They agreed to merge their organisations to create the National Resistance Movement (NRM), with an armed branch titled the National Resistance Army (NRA).[117] Although the military value of the UFF was marginal, this merger was a political masterstroke for Museveni and his PRA: while Lule was given the position of NRM Chairman, Museveni kept the position of Chairman of the NRA's High Command (which later included 12 people), de-facto granting himself undisputed control over the entire movement. Furthermore, Lule was older than Museveni and much more respected among the Buganda population. This was particularly important because the Buganda represented the majority in the strategic area known as the Luweero Triangle, composed of five districts and traversed by three major roads – where the PRA wanted to launch its 'people's war'. Furthermore, the majority of PRA leaders – including Museveni (a Hima from

Yoweri Kaguta Museveni while leading the NRA during the Bush War. (UPDF)

Youngster Fred Rwigyema – a child of Rwandan-Tutsi refugees who had lived in Uganda since the early 1960s – joined the NRA in 1981, and was appointed CO of its 5th Section. Seen here with a group of Western journalists, Rwigyema was to prove a highly effective and popular commander and enjoy a distinguished career, becoming Museveni's deputy. (UPDF)

A group of NRA insurgents in 1982. Although nearly all were wearing civilian clothes and armed with a wild miscellany of firearms, they proved far better indoctrinated and more disciplined than the UNLA. This was what eventually made them so successful during the Bush War. (UPDF)

One of the first 'heavy weapons' pressed into service by the NRA was this ZPU-4 14.5mm calibre quad machine gun captured form the UNLA. (UPDF)

the Ankole group[118]) – came from other ethnic groups than Bugandas, which meant they could now compete with such rival insurgent *organisations* as the Uganda Freedom Movement (UFM) that had found it easy to recruit in Luweero.While highly successful, Museveni's trip abroad – which was extended into December – resulted in one of the most serious crises ever faced by his movement. During the second half of 1981, the PRA expanded more than four-fold: from around 200 to more than 900 men. With the help of ambushes and landmines, it established several 'no-go zones' for UNLA troops and thus – for the first time – found itself in control of sizeable areas. The organisation meanwhile contained the homogenous core upon which it was built, consisting primarily of ex-FRONASA members of Ankole descent, but also ever larger numbers of newly-recruited Buganda. A number of well-educated volunteers who rallied to the group from Kampala tended to perceive themselves as natural leaders because of their academic background; they resented obeying orders from nearly-illiterate peasants, and also had social values almost opposite to those shared by the members with a military background. Naturally, this situation was bound to cause suspicions and tensions between these different groups, and these reached their climax when Sam Magara – Deputy Commander of the PRA – ordered a hasty trial and execution of a fighter who disappeared for few days without permission. This incident affected the mutual trust between insurgents and officers, some beginning to fear they would be summarily executed too.[119] Therefore, as soon as he was back, Museveni held a series of meetings among all the units, marking the beginning of a complete reorganisation of the PRA into the NRA, in the course of which he introduced a very detailed Code of Conduct, mandatory for all and strictly enforced. Henceforth, any crimes of murder, betrayal or rape fell under Category A and were punishable by death. Lesser offences fell under Category B and could be met with jail terms, demotion, suspension or corporal punishments.[120] The NRA later introduced the Operational Code of Conduct, drafted to deal with violations committed during operations (some of which could be dealt with on the spot) and which defined precisely the NRA's judicial system.[121]

Although still very small, the NRA then reorganised itself into six units: five of these were named after an African or Ugandan nationalist figure, with the other after the movement's early martyr, as detailed in Table 10.

Table 10: Organisation of the NRA, June 1981[122]

Unit	Commander
High Command	Yoweri Museveni
Kabalega Unit	Elly Tumwine
Mwanga Unit	Matayo Kyaligonza
Abdel Nasser Unit	Jack Muchunguzi
Nkrumah Unit	Fred Mwesigye
Mondlane Unit	Fred Rwigyema
Lutta Unit	Hannington Mugabi

To address problems with ranks of seniority, the NRA also introduced a new, simplified hierarchical system, as described in Table 11.

Table 11: Ranks of the NRA[123]

NRA Rank	Approximate Equivalent
Member of High Command (MHC)	Brigadier
Senior Officer (SO)	Major or Colonel
Junior Officer Class I (JOI)	Captain
Junior Officer Class II (JOII)	Lieutenant
Provisional Junior Officer II (P/JOII)	Sub-Lieutenant

Except for regular fighters, there was a small group of bodyguards responsible for protection of the leader.

A Text-Book People's War

At first glance, the majority of NRA fighters never looked very much like members of a well-organised military service. Most of them wore civilian clothes because the organisation could never afford to procure enough military fatigues and arms for all of its members. But their appearance was often deceptive, as the NRA figured high among the best-organised and most-disciplined insurgent movements ever in Africa.What the NRA did much better than other insurgent groups, and what eventually made it as successful as it became in this war, was good integration of its political and military strategies. Intense pressure of renewed and usually overwhelming UNLA offensives in 1983 forced its High Command to decline to defend its recently established 'safe zones'. While this left the local population with a choice of fleeing their homes or facing the wrath of government troops, even at this stage of the conflict such dramatic events were insufficient to break the very strong links between insurgents and the population – especially so in the Luweero Triangle. On the contrary, the inherent unpopularity of Obote and his military – made even worse by subsequent mass-executions committed by the UNLA and UPC-militias – resulted in civilians providing ever more support for the NRA. More importantly, although the NRA used a typical leftist vocabulary and was organised along 'classic' Leninist and Maoist patterns inherited from earlier liberation struggles, its ideology was first and foremost nationalistic: it never attempted to implement any kind of radical social changes (like land redistribution, for example). On the contrary, its attacks on police stations, members of the UPC and other government representatives usually resulted in local power vacuums. In order to fill this vacuum, the NRA began to encourage locals to run clandestine committees responsible for providing food, intelligence and to select new recruits. In order not to unnecessarily antagonise the communities in question, it usually picked elders or comparatively wealthy people from rural elites. By 1983, its clandestine committees were replaced by Resistance Committees (RCs), members of which were publicly elected by the local population – which was also in a position to revoke them.[124] This was nothing short of a true revolution – especially so in the formerly highly-centralised kingdom of Buganda, where the chieftains were always designated by the authorities. However, this process helped free the NRA from any responsibility for misconduct by members of the RCs. Members of the RCs in turn elected their representatives for parish and county levels, who in turn were sending their representatives to the National Resistance Council (NRC) – which was one of the most important bodies of the NRM and chaired by no less than Yoweri Museveni. Overall, while this system provided for minimal influence of local electors upon the hierarchy, it proved highly successful in raising the popularity of the NRA, fund-raising and recruiting – and, eventually, it proved instrumental in the movement's ultimate success.[125]

Indeed, over time, such policies made the insurgents so popular that the population began helping them by denouncing any government informers – usually recruited among the workers of northern origin established in the Triangle. The NRA not only very rarely executed any of its captives, but usually sent them to re-education camps where they could amend themselves before returning to their communities. It was seldom that the NRA felt forced to run covert operations to assassinate collaborators: thanks to superior intelligence, the insurgents proved capable of using Obote's security services to do the dirty job for them – for example by leaking manipulated intelligence to compromise the government's own informers.[126] By 1984, the insurgents successfully eliminated – whether by conversion, assassination or by simply forcing them to flee – nearly all of the government's sources of intelligence in their area of operations. Despite a few small-scale massacres allegedly committed in 1983, and being not adverse to targeted assassinations when other ways had failed, the NRA's policy was to take the greatest possible care to minimise casualties among civilians and protect its image among the public. In turn, any offences committed by insurgents were judged in front of the victims, in order to demonstrate the NRA's commitment and responsibility – but also its moral superiority over the UNLA and other insurgent groups.[127]Overall, Museveni's application of Mao's 'People's War' principles, mixed with a deep-rooted pragmatism, can only be described as a text-book example of a successful insurgency. The NRA never experienced difficulties with recruitment: apart from ex-FRONASA and UPM fighters, and recruits selected by the RCs in the Luweero Triangle, other significant sources of its manpower were added

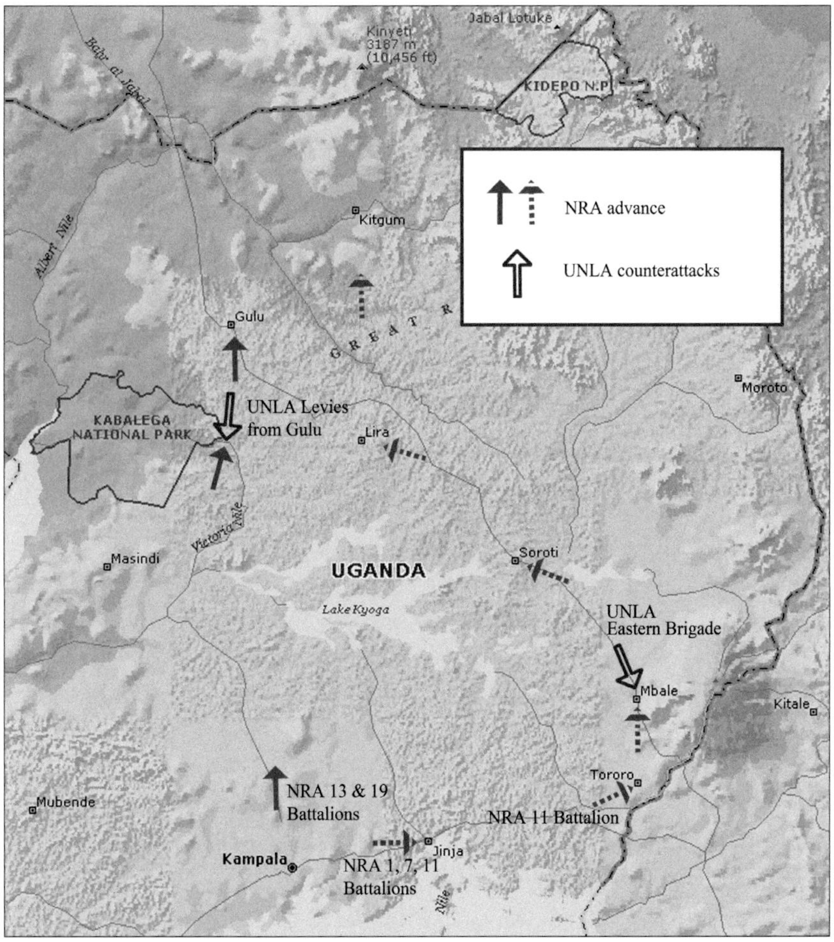

A map of the NRA's campaign in northern central Uganda after the capture of Kampala, in January–March 1986. (Tom Cooper)

by such actions of the government as unleashing the UPC Youth Wing against Rwandan Tutsi exiles present in Uganda since the early 1960s. Obote's administration perceived the Tutsi as 'natural NRA-collaborators' because of their historical connections to the Hima (Museveni's sub-group of the Ankole ethnic group). Unsurprisingly, this resulted in scores of young Rwandan exiles – most of whom were born and raised in Uganda – eagerly rallying around the NRA in order to get an opportunity to fight back, but also to gain the military skills necessary for their ultimate plan: a return to Rwanda. Rwandan Tutsis eventually made up to 20 percent of the NRA by early 1986.[128]Yet another source of manpower for the insurgents was also provided by the government. Random massacres committed by the UNLA in the Luweero Triangle from 1983 onwards left in their wake many orphans or children separated from their families. Most of them – often as young as four – found shelter with the NRA and became the *kadogos* ('little ones' in Swahili): child soldiers with limited military training, primarily used for scouting, as messengers or for guard duties.

Birth of a New Army

Generally, the NRA promulgated a dialogue-oriented culture with constant meetings at various levels, during which subordinates were left to openly criticise their superiors, while significant parts of the decision-making processes were decentralised.[129] Although chaired by a commanding officer, an administrative committee including all cadre was set up for every battalion, in charge of all important decision-making, as well as promotions. However, while the general strategy and standard tactics were known to everybody, the movement maintained operational confidentiality by systematically following the 'need to know' principle.[130]

To further improve its combat effectiveness and organisation, the NRA developed a dedicated training infrastructure – the Nkrumah Unit, to which all new recruits were assigned – and wrote its own infantry tactics and collective weapons training handbooks. The regimen was divided into two halves: the first dedicated to classic military training, and the second consisting of political education. Even after completion of primary training, new recruits were only gradually introduced to combat, in order to build self-confidence and experience.[131] Psychological warfare was pursued intensively too. The NRA's Code of Conduct made the removal of all friendly casualties a mandatory issue – with the aim of building a reputation of invincibility among enemy ranks. As a whole, this training system enabled the insurgency to grow from 900 men in December 1981 to more than 4,000 in early 1983, without losing cohesion or efficiency.[132]

Meanwhile, the force structure was further expanded through the creation of the First Mobile Force. This battalion-sized force included four companies (designated A, B, C and D), led by Fred Rwigyema and Salim Saleh (Museveni's brother). Controlled directly by the High Command, it was used to wage mobile warfare in areas not under NRA control and was the only unit granted permission to attack fortified positions and army barracks. Another major unit became the Abdel Nasser Task Force, a 50-man strong outfit nicknamed the 'Black Bombers'. Led by Matayo Kyaligonza (a former SRB operative), it primarily attacked police stations, army bases and installations of economic importance around Kampala.

Luke-Warm Support from Libya

The major problem of the NRA during 1982 remained the fact that – contrary to other contemporary insurgent groups elsewhere in Africa – it lacked not only a major foreign supporter, but also a secure base in a neighbouring country where it could provide training for its fighters, and from which it could run logistical support. The Ugandan Bush-War failed to attract attention from major powers and did not evolve into a typical, Cold-War-era confrontation between the East and the West. No matter how precious, even the British support for Obote's administration remained very limited by nature. It was only Libyan leader Gaddafi who attempted to regain some influence in the Ugandan political scene through the provision of arms to various insurgent groups. Museveni travelled to Libya in mid-1981, but his trip produced only limited results as Gaddafi advocated a union of all the major insurgent groups which were fighting against Obote. With the NRA considering the UFM and UNRF as rivals rather than allies, this idea was anything but welcome – although various Ugandan insurgent leaders, eager to get some support, pretended to follow the *Rais'* lead by forming the ephemeral and actually fictional Ugandan People's Front (UPF). Unsurprisingly, Gaddafi cancelled his low-profile support in 1982 after smuggling only about 800 rifles and machine guns, a few RPG-7s and some landmines into the Luweero Triangle in August 1981.[133]

James Kashilingi was one of only two professional officers to join the NRA early on. Trained as a commando officer in Iraq during Amin's rule, he went on to save Museveni on at least one occasion during the Bush War, only to be arrested and imprisoned over inter-NRA disputes in the 1990s. (UPDF)

Museveni's brother, Salim Saleh, also joined the NRA and was in charge of several units during the Bush War. (UPDF)

Major-General David Oyite Ojok, certainly the most popular and trusted commander of the UNLA, was killed in a crash in an AB.412 helicopter near Kasozi on 2 December 1982. (UPDF)

Luweero Triangle

Although internally strong, the weakly-armed NRA thus found itself facing great odds when the UNLA launched its first major attempt to crush the insurgency in the Luweero Triangle in May and June 1982. This enterprise, code-named Operation Bonanza, involved five UNLA battalions led by the Chief of Staff, Major-Genaral Oyite Ojok, supported by police units primarily consisting of northern Ugandans. Opting to defend its major zone of influence, the NRA initially managed to beat back all of their attacks. Some of the fiercest fighting occurred around the Kalongero Bridge, which the UNLA troops had to pass during their advance on the insurgent HQ in Semuto. Because of the obvious importance of this bridge, it was defended by a reinforced company of the First Mobile Force which beat back repeated assaults by the Central Brigade, supported by mortars, causing heavy casualties to NYA militiamen who advanced without taking cover, in so-called 'open-chest march' (Kifuwa Wazi). Elsewhere, the UNLA's attempt to make use of counter-ambush tactics while advancing into areas under NRA control met with very little success, as government troops were insufficiently trained for this task and were usually detected in time by insurgents. Operation Bonanza thus ended in failure, but not before the UNLA repeated its performance from the West Nile and began imposing collective punishment on residents, virtually depopulating much of the region as any who did not flee were killed. The sheer extent of brutalities was best illustrated during an insurgent attack on Kakiri, a few months after the end of the offensive, when, after assaulting their objective, NRA fighters found the Army's positions empty – 'occupied' only by bodies of countless dead. Unsurprisingly, by the end of 1982, the NRA was in control of an area about 10,000km^2 in size, populated by about one million.[134]

After defeating the UNRF and UFM in late 1982, the government ordered the UNLA into a new offensive against the NRA in January 1983. Deploying between 4,000 and 7,000 troops supported by D-30 howitzers, M-46 cannons and MRLS, the military attempted to force the NRA out of densely-populated and fertile areas on the northern side of the Luweero Triangle into the less-hospitable southern side, mainly inhabited by cattle-herders.[135] Tactics applied during this operation involved sending an overwhelming force into the targeted zone to establish garrisons to maintain control and then to start interdicting the NRA with random artillery shelling.The insurgents proved unable to stop this onslaught, instead attempting to hit back with attacks into the enemy rear, but suffered extensive losses in the process. For example, the so-called 'First Team' – the elite D Company of the First Mobile Force – was badly beaten up during an attack on Bukalabi on 21 February. Despite good reconnaissance, the insurgents led by Salim Saleh ended in the middle of a carefully-laid 'killing ground', established by a well-trained and disciplined UNLA unit that changed its positions only a few hours before the attack. As a result, nine NRA were killed in a matter of minutes, several others – including Saleh – wounded, and the company had to beat a hasty retreat.

Safari 50

Unacustomed to heavy casualties, this defeat came as a rude shock for the NRA, but worse was to follow. In May 1983, Museveni led in person a single column of 1,500 fighers who marched for 322km (200 miles) to reach their target: the Kabamba Training Camp. The entire plan began to collapse during this manoeuvre. Inexperienced in planning operations involving such large units, the leader of the NRA overestimated the pace at which the column could advance and therefore the food supplies it had to carry. Instead of reaching their target within five to seven days, the insurgents arrived at their destination only after two weeks, by when their food supplies were used up. As exhaustion and hunger resulted in numerous cases of indiscipline and even desertion, and offences were usually punished with 50 cane-lashes, the operation became known as 'Safari 50' among the fighters involved. Eventually, although reaching their designation, Museveni called off the operation, concluding his insurgents were much too weak to face any unforeseen events. The NRA thus withdrew into the northern part of the Luweero Triangle, leaving behind only a small party near Kampala.[136]As thousands of civilians expressed their wish to go with them, their exodus and re-settlement had to be organised too, in the course of which the insurgents attempted to delay a UNLA advance as long as possible while civilians were marching along pre-defined routes to the Singo area. While this operation was concluded successfully, it ended with Museveni, his fighters and tens of thousands of people cornered in an area that could not support them with the necessary food: the peninsula surrounded by the rivers Mayanja, Lugogo and Kafu, where the NRA excelled in using riverbeds as killing grounds. The UNLA contented itself to laying siege to the zone with the help of a ring of positions around it. Although repeatedly infiltrating enemy positions to harvest cassavaplants, insurgent attempts to establish production units and grow their own food largely failed. For the time being, the NRA was thus highly dependent on the provision of support from its clandestine network of sympathisers around the country.[137]

One of the few Agusta-Bell AB.205s operated by the UNLA during the early 1980s. Although providing valuable service, the fleet was much too small and too hampered by the de-facto US arms embargo, but was to prove effective in combat against NRA insurgents. (Albert Grandolini Collection)

The grim scene from one of many ossuaries in the Luweero Triangle: most of the bones collected there belonged to victims of government repression. (Fausto Biloslavo)

Turning the Tide

During the second half of 1983, the insurgents managed to re-infiltrate into their original area of operations; they further expanded the area under their control and captured plenty of arms in a number of minor clashes. On 2 December, the UNLA suffered a particularly devastating blow when an AB.412 helicopter crashed near Kasozi, killing Major-Genaral David Oyite Ojok, its most popular officer, well-liked and trusted by Acholi and Langi alike. Worse yet, Obote needed months to find a replacement, and the figure in question – Brig Smith Opon Acak – while competent enough, not only did not poses Ojok's charisma but also failed to prevent subsequent divisions in the military.Another negative consequence of this loss was that the UNLA remained passive for most of 1983 and early 1984, enabling the NRA to expand its main strike force – the First Mobile Force – into the Mobile Brigade, consisting of small battalions, each of which included 75 weapons, and three unarmed support companies. The first major operation of the Mobile Brigade was aimed at the Masindi Artillery School. This objective, far away from the combat zone, was carefully reconnoitred for weeks and infiltrated by insurgents who found a garrison with lax security measures. The first attack on Masindi was aborted because the insurgent column was detected well before reaching its designation. The second attempt, however, proved much more successful.It began on the evening of 19 February 1984, when the 1st, 3rd and 5th Battalions of the Mobile Brigade (the 7th Battalion acted as reserve) started a march of 110km (68 miles) towards their objective. They covered this distance, alternating runs and quick walks, within less than 48 hours, arriving in the vicinity of Masindi early on the morning of 20 February. After seizing the undefended Kigulya Hill, which dominated the camp, they launched an assault which took the garrison completely by surprise. Most of the UNLA troops fled after offering only token resistance. Using captured trucks, the Mobile Brigade left the area around midday, taking plenty of firearms and ammunition with it, although leaving behind a number of D-30 howitzers. All vehicles were subsequently abandoned when the Brigade met another detachment that helped it haul the booty back to NRA bases. Lame UNLA attempts to launch a pursuit were easily beaten back and the insurgents suffered a loss of only one KIA during the operation, while causing more than 50 casualties to the government – including a number of Tanzanian instructors who were captured and later sent back home with a message for President Nyerere. It is sufficient to observe that thanks to capturing 765 rifles and machine guns, the NRA's fire-power was nearly doubled.[138]In another similar raid against the town of Hoima, on 1 June, the insurgents not only captured additional arms, but also robbed the local bank, in effect re-financing themselves. Such success emboldened Museveni, and in late 1984 he decided to launch a third attempt against the Kabamba Training Camp.This time a column of 1,400 troops of the Mobile Brigade was detected by the UPC quite early, and the NRA High Command therefore decided to split its force into two elements. Acting as a decoy and consisting of several minor units, Museveni's command marched into the area between Bukomero (on the Kampala–Hoima road) and Kyamusisi (on the Mityana–Bukuya road). Museveni's brother, meanwhile, led the Mobile Brigade straight for Kabamba, reaching it on 31 December after a seven-day march. Instead of celebrating New Year's Eve, the insurgents took some rest and then attacked at 10 a.m. on 1 January 1985. Most of the garrison was quickly overrun because the trenches surrounding it were unoccupied. However, one UNLA soldier locked himself inside the armoury and single-handedly held up the insurgents for five hours – until he was blown up by a landime thrown through the entrance. Fortunately for everyone else, the detonation failed to ignite the extensive ammunition stocks, and the NRA thus seized a booty of 650 rifles, five machine guns, one 60mm calibre mortar, 90,000 rounds of ammunition, 493 hand- and anti-tank grenades, 70 mortar shells and 124 RPG-rounds. The delay caused by the unforeseen resistance in the armoury allowed the UNLA garrison in nearby Mubende to advance on Kabamba, but this column was easily ambushed by the 1st Battalion Mobile Brigade and forced to withdraw. The NRA then retreated too, re-uniting with Museveni's column a few days later.[139]Furious at this defeat, Brig Acak ordered a pursuit, and his troops caught the Mobile Brigade while it was camping in the Birembo Primary School on 12 January. Several infantry teams probed the camp atop a hill before it was subjected to an artillery barrage that killed five bodyguards of the High Command, but other insurgents managed to exfiltrate and rally within the NRA-controlled territory before the government was able to block and encircle them.

Running Battle

The successful conclusion of this long-range raid behind government lines proved not only a morale-booster but enabled the NRA to expand its structure to six mobile battalions equipped with 300 firearms each, and then dispatch two of these to reinforce local fighters, but also keep one as a reserve (for details of insurgent organisation at this time, see Table 12). While entrusting Fred Rwigyema with the task of realising his long-delayed project of opening a 'second front', Museveni felt safe enough for another trip abroad to search for international support in March 1985. Rwigyema left the Luweero Triangle, leading the 11th Battalion on a long march to the Ruwenzori Mountains on 30 March. His column included a number of loyal civilians, some sick and walking wounded.

Table 12: NRA Mobile Forces, early 1985

Unit	Assignement
1st Battalion	Mobile Brigade
3rd Battalion	Mobile Brigade
5th Battalion	Mobile Brigade
7th Battalion	independent
9th Battalion	independent
11th Battalion	reserve

Meanwhle, Acak appointed Lieutenant-Colonel John Ogole as the new commander of UNLA units fighting the NRA in the Luweero Triangle. While also lacking Ojok's charisma, Ogole proved an aggressive officer, excellently prepared for his task. Trained at Fort Leavenwroth, he commanded the Special Anti-Banditry Brigade (later re-designated 50 Special Brigade), which consisted of four battalions of 5,000 hand-picked officers and other ranks, well-supported by artillery and MRLS.[140] What Ogole also lacked was tactical ideas; although his unit was more potent than any of those previously deployed against the NRA, it still followed the same pattern of advancing into the targeted area and digging-in in the hope that the insurgents would attack it and expose themselves to superior fire-power.[141]Nevertheless, the vivid activity of the Mobile Brigade sooner or later had to result in a collision with the crack UNLA unit. This occurred in June 1985, when a battalion of the Special Brigade began tracking one of the NRA units which was marched out of the Ngoma area. All the counter-tracking methods applied by insurgents failed and the UNLA battalion was soon reinforced by another unit, while the third battalion of the Special Brigade entrenched itself behind the River Mayanja, turning the operation into a classic 'hammer and anvil' one. Learning about this deployment ahead of them, the commanders of the Mobile Brigade chose to turn against their pursuers and offer battle on the evening of 20 June. Their units established an L-shaped ambush down the axis of the enemy's advance. The base of this formation was occupied by the 3rd Battalion, reinforced by the Brigade's RPGs and machine guns; the 5th Battalion took position along the flank, while the 1st Battalion remained as reserve behind the 2nd Battalion and Brigade HQ.The two UNLA battalions resumed their advance on the morning of 21 June, and their company-sized vanguard ran straight into an ambush, losing 50 KIA in the process. The Special Brigade took about an hour to reorganise and re-assess its situation before launching a methodical infantry assault supported by accurate mortar- and machine-gun fire. After two hours of fighting, Salem Saleh was forced to reinforce the 3rd Battalion with the 1st, but then the UNLA nearly outflanked the entire position and only a rapid intervention of the 5th Battalion saved the day. Sensing the enemy wavering, the insurgents finally launched a general counter-attack and routed the government troops in the course of a pursuit that last until dusk. This hard-fought battle ended in a clear-cut NRA victory: not only did it cause between 200 and 300 casualties in exchange for just 23 of its own KIA, but the defeat of a crack unit delivered a massive psychological blow to the entire UNLA.[142]

Fall of Milton Obote

Combined with the death of Major-Genaral Ojok, and successive and significant casualties in combat against insurgents, the defeat of the Special Brigade completely disrupted the UNLA's cohesion. Acholi soldiers – which formed the majority of the ranks, but felt neglected while doing most of the fighting and dying – mutinied in Jinja in June 1985 upon receiving the order to re-deploy to Fort Portal. Troops based in Mbuya barracks openly disobeyed orders issued by Acak. The rift rapidly expanded to within the highest ranks of the military when the Democratic Party – which lacked its own armed wing – attempted to exploit the opportunity to gain influence in the military. Still recalling what happened

Freshly-recruited *kadogo* of the NRA during a parade in Kampala, shortly after the Ugandan capital was captured by insurgents in January 1986. They were soon to become a prominent feature on battlefields not only in Uganda, but in several neighbouring countries too. (Fausto Biloslavo)

Yoweri Museveni (centre, with light uniform) with top NRA commanders shortly after taking over in Kampala. Fred Rwigyema – his deputy, of Rwandan origin – is first to his left. (UPDF)

with Acholi troops immediately after Amin's coup, Bajilio Olara Okello ordered his brigade from Gulu to march on Kampla. Benefitting from the indirect support of the NRA – which let his column pass through an area controlled by insurgents – Okello entered the capital while facing minimal resistance (although not without losing one of only two M4 Shermans that were still in service), and toppled Obote's government on 27 July.[143]While Tito Okello was appointed the new Head of State – with Bajilio Okello as Army Chief of Staff – the new government immediately opened negotiations with various political and insurgent groups, proposing to them the establishment of a government of national unity. Following protracted negotiations, a corresponding agreement was signed in August, resulting in the establishment of a Military Council which included representatives of the Federal Democratic Movement of Uganda (FEDEMU, led by Dr Andrew Kayira) and the UFM, but also the FUNA and the UNRF. These groups occupied five out of 12 seats in the government, while the rest was held by the UNLA.For ideological reasons – mainly Museveni's desire to completely overhaul the Ugandan political system – the NRA decided to stay out of the National Unity government and to continue the war. However, to buy time, Museveni appeared at peace talks in Nairobi, sponsored by the Kenyan president, which began on 26 August. These led to a treaty on 17 December, which envisioned the reorganisation of the UNLA under the supervision of foreign parties, free elections and Museveni's appointment as Vice-Chairman of the Military Council. Eventually, all the negotiations and the treaty became completely irrelevant, when the NRA High Command meanwhile ordered its units to end the de-facto truce and resume military operations, aiming for a complete defeat of all of its rivals. In a carefully orchestrated blow, the insurgents simultaneously attacked and overran the garrisons at Busunju, Kiboga, Luweero and Matuga in the Triangle: most of the troops were captured without a fight, disarmed and then sent to Kampala on 24 August 1986. In Western Uganda, the 11th Battalion captured Fort Portal, while the Mobile Brigade captured the towns of Bokasa, Hoima, Mityana, Mubende and Wakiso by the end of September, putting the NRA in control of all of central and western Uganda, together with border crossings to Rwanda and Zaire.[144]

Decisive Battles

What was left of the UNLA in late 1986 was two brigades and a miscellany of support units – altogether about 12,000 troops – securing Kampala, and two reinforced regiments in southern Uganda – each about 2,000–3,000 strong – which withdrew into the garrisons of Mbarara and Masaka. The NRA High Command decided to invest both of the later targets before advancing on the capital.The first attack on Mbarara ended with the costliest defeat ever suffered by the NRA. The 11th Battalion advanced straight into the town and captured the military base against minimal resistance, because the UNLA troops there ran away. As usual in such cases, the insurgents began retrieving equipment, arms and ammunition, but this time they also neglected taking protective measures. This proved a fatal mistake because the garrison in Mbarara was led by a particularly aggressive and resourceful officer whom they had not encountered until that time: Lieutenant-Colonel Santansio Constantine Otto. Otto remained near the town and, after regrouping his troops, launched a counter-attack that took the 11th Battalion completely by surprise and inflicted 45 casualties. The beaten NRA unit was forced to withdraw from Mbarara and entrench in the hills surrounding the town, waiting for reinforcements in the form of the 9th Battalion. This resulted in a classic siege, in the course of which Otto's garrison successfully maintained its hold on the barracks, part of the town and several surrounding villages, which provided it with at least a limited supply of food. Kampala immediately dispatched a battalion-sized column from Masaka, but this unit was routed by the Mobile Brigade in an ambush set up between Lyantonde and Mbarara. A few days later, on 24 September, the NRA assaulted Masaka, but its first attempt was beaten back by defenders well-protected in fortifications which controlled several minefields, and supported by heavy 14.5mm calibre machine guns, 37mm calibre anti-aircraft cannons and 120mm calibre mortars.[145]

Museveni's commanders then split their forces: the 3rd Battalion was sent to reinforce the 9th and 11th near Mbarara, while the 1st and 5th entrenched at the northern end of the Katonga bridge – on the northern side of the 20km (12 mile) causeway stretching from Nabusanke in the north to Lukaya. Determined to reopen the only direct road between Kampala and Masaka, the UNLA deployed its 11th Battalion, supported by several batteries of light artillery and MRLS, and a detachment of FUNA troops. Additional support was provided by helicopters which were used to drop light bombs on defenders. After several days of unsuccessful frontal attacks, government troops finally came up with the idea to cross the swamp camouflaged by floating papyrus and hit the NRA in the flank, in support of a frontal assault with the help of an APC. While this attempt failed too, the OT-64 passed the bridge, but insurgent fire scattered the accompanying infantry. Concluding it was left on its own, the crew eventually abandoned the vehicle and it was later burned out by the NRA.[146]

Meanwhile, the Masaka Mechanised Regiment of the UNLA launched a series of attacks against the 3rd Battalion NRA, but all were repulsed. The last attempt, undertaken on 31 September, was led by Major Tebandeke, who was killed in the course of the action. His successor, Captain Olanya Ojara, ordered the survivors to withdraw and only defend. Already shaken by all the fighting, the 3rd Battalion NRA followed in fashion and contented itself with hermetically sealing the siege of the garrison, only randomly harassing it with mortar fire. Before long, Ojara's unit began succumbing to indiscipline and internal rifts, reaching the point where everybody was regrouped along ethnic lines. The UNLA attempted to provide the garrison with supplies dropped from helicopters, but most of these were driven off by heavy – although inaccurate – anti-aircraft fire.[147] Eventually, around 3,000 semi-starved troops surrendered on 12 December 1985, providing the NRA with a huge cache of arms and ammunition. Reinforced, the insurgents then concentrated all of their efforts against Mbarara, which surrendered in January 1986.[148]

Undisturbed Advance on Kampala

During the sieges of Mbarara and Masaka, the NRA was able to significantly expand through the infusion of up to 9,000 volunteers who completed their training in December 1985. This influx of manpower was used to create four new battalions and a support unit equipped with 14.5mm calibre machine guns, 37mm calibre anti-aircraft cannons and heavy mortars. Defecting UNLA troops also provided three Soviet-made BTR-60 APCs.Despite such a massive build-up, the insurgency maintained discipline by carefully selecting its new fighters from among the ranks of numerous volunteers eager to rally to the winning party, and thanks to its highly-efficient training system. However, while the training of new fighters was within its ability, expanding the core of battle-hardened and proven commanders was not. Therefore, instead of increasing the number of units, the NRA increased their size: from 600 men to approximately 1,500 per battalion. Only two new formations were established – the 19th and the 21st Battalions, each totalling 1,900 combatants.[149] Correspondingly, by late January 1986, the NRA's organisational structure was as detailed in Table 13.

Table 13: NRA Order of Battle, January 1986[150]

Unit	Commanding Officer
Special Force	Jet Mwebaze
1st Battalion	Pecos Kutesa
3rd Battalion	Patrick Lumumba
5th Battalion	Steven Kashaka
7th Battalion	Matayo Kyaligonza
9th Battalion	Julius Chihandae
11th Battalion	Chefe Ali
13th Battalion	Yvan Koreta
15th Battalion	Samson Mande
19th Battalion	Peter Kerim
21st Battalion	Benon Tumukunde

With such a force behind them, Museveni and the High Command were finally able to plan the operation for the seizure of Kampala. Planned during a meeting at the Masaka Sports Club, the offensive began in mid-January 1986, with insurgents rapidly advancing from several directions to within 15km of the city centre, while the 9th and 19th Battalions blocked the Masinda–Hoima Road to prevent any counter-attacks by UNLA units still active in northern Uganda. The final offensive on Kampala was by far the largest-ever operation undertaken by the NRA. It included six battalions and the Special Force, totalling about 9,600 men.

The operation began with infiltration of NRA's child soldiers – so-called *kadogo* – into Kampala, as recalled by one eyewitnesses:

My friends told me Okello made a deal with some organisation named Uganda Freedom Army, which included plenty of kadogo. They were settled in our part of Kampala and we soon saw these kids on the streets, wearing civilian clothes all the time, hanging around – but especially around places where there were any UNLA troops. They would earn from filling holes in the roads (Kampala roads were awful at the time because of 15 years of no maintenance) ... but later we understood these kids were there to watch what the UNLA was doing ... when it was all over, we never heard of that organisation again. It vanished ... Generally, it was hard to tell the difference between that Uganda Freedom Army and the NRA, anyway:

they were better organised and disciplined than the UNLA. Only the slim and tall guys of the NRA made the difference ... many of their officers were Batutis-Rwandans and very few of them could speak French.[151]

With its troops in place and after obtaining necessary intelligence about UNLA deployment around the city, the actual NRA attack began with the 1st, 3rd, 7th and 11th Battalions approaching Kampala from the west. They captured such objectives as the Bugesa crossroads, Lubiri and Makindye barracks, the Radio Uganda Building and Republic House – the latter positioned on the highest hill in the capital. Meanwhile, the 5th, 13th and the Special Force Battalion occupied blocking positions between Kampala and Entebbe, along the roads to Masindi and to Jinja. By accident, during the following battle, the Special Force was re-assigned the task of supporting the 13th Battalion and thus left one road open forthe retreat of the UNLA.[152]After a few days of continuous advance against often fierce resistance by UNLA and FUNA units, the NRA seized the Bugesa crossroads, due to the government troops failing to occupy the nearby Muttundwe Hill. The latter was promptly secured and the insurgents emplaced most of their anti-aircraft cannons and mortars there.The final assault into Kampala was launched on 24 January. Generally, the poorly motivated and led UNLA units offered weak resistance; most FUNA troops either defected or sided with the NRA. The only serious battle during this campaign began on the evening of 25 January when the 7th Battalion encountered a cohesive defence system – including machine guns emplaced to cover all avenues of approach – in Makindye barracks. It took the insurgents two days of heavy fighting to overcome resistance within the complex. Elsewhere, taking advantage of support from heavy weapons emplaced atop the Muttundwe Hill, the 11th Battalion captured the Kololo Summit View, neutralizing the UNLA's artillery positioned there, during the morning of 26 January. This action also enabled the 1st Battalion to capture the Radio Uganda Building (losing one BTR-60 and one 37mm calibre anti-aircraft cannon in the process). Another problematic situation developed in the south, where the 5th Battalion NRA found itself confronted by a reinforced battalion of UNLA troops which advanced from Entebbe towards Kampala. The government troops managed to breach the insurgent line, forcing the High Command NRA to re-direct the 3rd Battalion in this direction. The latter encircled the Army unit and forced all of its 900 troops to surrender. Eventually, about 9,000 government troops escaped from Kampala with their families, using the few roads the Special Force NRA left open because of a faulty order. The insurgents suffered a loss of 20 KIA, in exchange for killing 80 enemy troops and capturing nearly 3,000.[153]

CHAPTER FIVE:
CONQUEST OF THE NORTH

Immediately after the fall of Kampala, and amid preparations for Museveni to be sworn in as the new President of Uganda (on 29 January 1986), all available NRA contingents were dispatched for the pursuit of retreating UNLA units in the direction of Jinja and Gulu.The 1st, 7th and 11th Battalions advanced on Jinja and secured the town by the end of January. They repeated the exercise in Tororo a few days later, against rather disorganised delaying actions by retreating UNLA elements. It was at this point that a last-ditch-attempt was made by several top Army officers to reorganise some of their fleeing units and defend the north of Uganda. Civilians at Gulu and Kitgum were hurriedly trained and provided with arms taken from local armouries, under the supervision of Lieutenant Gen Bazilio Olara-Okello, then rushed into positions at Kamdini Falls in an attempt to prevent the NRA from crossing the Nile River. Meanwhile, Lieutenant-Colonel Kenneth Kilama – CO of UNLA's Eastern Brigade – launched a counter-attack on Tororo: while futile, this attempt delayed the NRA's two-pronged advance on Gulu. Eventually, the 13th and 19th Battalions crossed the Nile after causing heavy casualties to the defenders, while the 11th Battalion moved on Soroti after a fierce battle with UNLA elements at the Manafa River. In the light of this series of defeats, the UNLA collapsed and thousands of its officers and other ranks fled over the border to Sudan, or simply went back to their villages.[154]

Early in March, the 1st Battalion joined the 13th and the 19th while taking Gulu and Kitgum, and continued the advance right up to the border, nominally asserting the new government's control over all of Uganda.Back in Kampala, the NRM began implementing its agenda of refurbishing the entire political and security system of the country. All political parties were forbidden, described as vehicles of tribalism and division, and thus responsible for the decades of ruinous civil wars and unrest that had plagued Uganda. A de-centralised government system was introduced instead, which saw an expansion of the Resistance Council system to all corners of the country.

From Nra To Updf

Despite having around 20,000 troops under arms by February 1986, the NRA was still too small to effectively control the whole of Uganda – even more so as it had to take over, at least temporarily, the tasks of the police too. Therefore, Museveni almost immediately began expanding his army, resulting in a build-up that increased it by five-fold during the following years.The High Command Unit became a battalion-sized force renamed as the Presidential Protection Unit, while the NRA established about a dozen new battalions and three brigade headquarters in March and April. The post-1986 build-up was a kind of a trade-off. To limit

Yoweri Museveni was sworn in as the new President of Uganda on 29 January 1986. While his politics stabilised the country and resulted in a gradual economic recovery, it would take years longer to end the different insurgencies in northern Uganda. (Fausto Biloslavo)

Alice Lauma Lakwena, a self-declared medium who led the HSMF insurgency in Uganda. (*monitor.co.uk*)

Major General Fred Rwigyema – the NRA's second in command – led the NRA's Mobile Brigade into a counter-attack on the HSMF in the Lira area in mid-January 1987, which marked the beginning of the end of the insurgency led by Alice Lakwena. (UPDF)

Joseph Kony, leader of the United Holy Salvation Army (later the Lord's Resistance Army), notorious for mass-hijackings and mutilations of civilians in northern Uganda. (Mark Lepko Collection)

the number of former enemies who might rally to new insurgent groups, but also to exploit the meanwhile sizeable pool of already trained soldiers, the NRA began recruiting thousands of former UNLA, FUNA, FEDEMO, UNRF and UFM combatants. To ease the process of their integration, they were usually grouped into homogenous groups according to their ancient affiliation. Some units even kept their former commanders. This is how the 25th, 31st and 33rd Battalions (ex-UNLA), the 27th Battalion (ex-FEDEMO) and the 35th Battalion (ex-UFM) came into being. Obviously, this practice generated a gap between carefully selected veteran NRA figthers, patiently trained and indoctrinated over the years, and new formations which had much lower standards of discipline and combat effectiveness. The expansion also put immense strain on the limited pool of experienced officers, very few of whom were experienced in conducting operations with large units. Such factors were to become primary reasons for the fast deteorioration of the NRA's behaviour – already apparent during very demanding COIN operations in Acholiland, between March and August 1986. Unsurprisingly, the new Ugandan military was quick in setting up an elaborate training structure with support from Cuba, Libya and the USA, but also the Anglo-Ugandan-South African joint-venture named Saracen Co. This expansion necessitated the abandonment of guerrilla-style ranks and introduction of a conventional pattern, but overall it changed little of the NRA's character. Essentially, it remained a light infantry force poorly equipped with heavy weapons, although the artillery regiment came into being in late 1986 and the mechanised regiment was established in 1987 (using a miscellany of tanks left behind from the UA and UNLA times, and 18 BTR-60s delivered by Libya and the Soviet Union).[155]

A Divisional structure was introduced in 1986, with the creation of the 4th Division, while the 2nd Division came into being in 1991. Meanwhile, the small flying component used five re-activated Bell and Agusta-Bell helicopters left over from the UNLA, but also two SIAI Marchetti SF.260WL light-strikers provided by Libya. This nucleus was reinforced through the acquisition of six Mil Mi-8T helicopters from the Soviet Union in 1987, although it took several years longer to build-up a core of trained Ugandan pilots and mechanics: even by 1994, all the personnel of the Air Wing still totalled barely 100.[156]Although dependent on substantial foreign aid, Kampala was spending more than a third of the national budget for defence purposes throughout this period. This caused severe pressure from different foreign donors and the World Bank, prompting Museveni to significantly reduce his military spending – primarily through drastically reducing the size of the military, from 90,000 in 1992 to about 50,000 in 1995.[157] Combined with substantial economic growth since the NRM took over, and ever increasing foreign aid (which on average made up to 15 percent of the Gross National Income between 1987 and 1995), Kampala managed to purchase a batch of T-55 MBTs via the Israeli company Silver Shadow in 1994, followed by dozens of South African-made Buffel and Mamba mine-resistant/ambush protected (MRAP) vehicles in 1995. During the same year, Uganda adopted a new constitution, resulting in the re-designation of the NRA into the Ugandan People's Defence Force (UPDF).[158]

Chaos in Acholiland

The proclamation of the NRM government did not bring an

end to the various armed conflicts that had devastated Uganda since 1978. On the contrary, dozens of new insurgent groups became active in the late 1980s. Although most enjoyed only very limited support of the local population (indeed, the majority of movements in question were little more than armed gangs which never represented a serious threat), the appearance of relatively large and well-organised insurgencies in Acholiland and Teso in northern Uganda did cause a serious crisis.To begin with, the populations of the Acholiland and Teso District were surprised by the appearance of disciplined NRA troops. Most of the families of UNLA soldiers even soon felt safe enough to return to their homes.[159] Nevertheless, different factors weighed heavily against a lasting peace in this region. Foremost was the deep mistrust between southerners – who composed the bulk of the NRA – who saw the Acholi soldiers, and Acholi people as a whole, as the main culprits of the UNLA's atrocities committed in the Luweero Triangle. In turn, many Acholi felt bitter over what they perceived as Museveni's betrayal of Okello, the only Acholi who ever rose to the presidential position in Uganda. Civilian elites lost their access to governmental positions as a result of the change of power, and the NRA victory had a devastating economic impact upon Acholiland and Teso, traditional suppliers of manpower for the military and security apparatus who were now without jobs. The NRM government then made a major mistake by dissolving various local militias raised since 1979 to protect the population against endemic cattle-raiding by the Karamojong agro-pastoral herders: related crimes reached entirely new proportions when this group gained access to large stocks of firearms by plundering abandoned UA armouries during the chaos which followed the Tanzanian invasion. Since the NRA proved unable to keep the Karamojong in check, the defenceless districts of Gulu, Kitgum and Teso were hit by a wave of cattle-raiding to the point where virtually all local herders were economically ruined within less than a year. This happened as thousands of former UNLA soldiers returned home; many found it difficult to return to peasantry and began to use weapons to make a living by plundering their kin.[160] The behaviour of NRA troops garrisoned in these three districts became progressively more brutal, although there was actually only one specific unit which ruined the Army's reputation: the 35th Battalion.Formed from former UFM insurgents, this unit began arbitrarily arresting and torturing civilians almost immediately after arriving in its new base. When, on 10 May 1986, all former UNLA soldiers were ordered to report and hand over their arms to the NRA, fear spread that the new authorities would massacre everybody who would appear. Many preferred to run into the bush instead.Therefore, it was local context, associated with economic disruption, the massive increase of armed robberies, presence of numerous men with previous military experience and the availability of small arms and ammunition, but mainly a deep mistrust between the new authorities and the population, that provided fertile ground for a resurgence of armed violence.

A company of the NRA's '*kadogo*' child soldiers. (Fausto Biloslavo)

A group of UPDA fighters encouraging themselves with a dance prior to battle. (Fausto Biloslavo)

Enter the UPDA

A new armed group named Uganda's People Democratic Army (UPDA), led by Eric Otema Alimadi (former Prime Minister in Obote's government), came together inside Sudan in July 1986.[161]

A column of UPDA fighters fording a creek in northern Uganda. Mostly consisting of ex-UNLA troops with significant combat experience, this group attracted almost soley Acholi and even fewer outside supporters. (Fausto Biloslavo)

Another photograph from the same series, revealing more details about 'uniforms' and armament of UPDA fighters, most of whom were armed with AK-47s of different origin and RPG-7s. (Fausto Biloslavo)

It launched its first offensive into Uganda, deploying between 3,000 and 4,000 combatants for an attack on the NRA garrison in Bibia, on 19 August. After suffering over 200 casualties, this assault was abandoned, but another UPDA element meanwhile advanced in the direction of Gulu, intending to use it as a springboard for an advance on Kampala.[162] Heading south, the UPDA assaulted Namokora, clashing with the 35th Battalion, on 28 August –this only a few days after the NRA unit went on a rampage that ended with the murder of 71 civilians. The 35th Battalion beat back the insurgents, but they returned on 14 September, forcing the NRA to abandon the town and beat a hasty retreat along the Namokora–Kitgum road. On its way, the unit was subjected to a number of ambushes in which it suffered at least 20 casualties.[163]Despite this success, the UPDA's plan backfired and the campaign soon degenerated into a classic insurgency as the NRA maintained a tight hold on all the towns, leaving the insurgents in control of only rural areas.[164] Furthermore, while the UPDA proved popular amongst the Acholi during the first months of its existence, it was deprived of an effective internal and external support, and lacked the necessary discipline. Therefore, although the troops of the 35th Battalion NRA continued with their atrocities against the local population, and although the UPDA established a number of units with impressive names (for full order of battle of this group in 1986–1988, see Table 14), the insurgent capabilities degenerated too.

Table 14: UPDA Order of Battle, 1986–1988[165]

Unit	Commanding Officer
Division 'One'	Lieutenant-Colonel John Angelo Okello (in 1988)
50th Brigade	
60th Brigade	
70th Brigade	Lieutenant-Colonel Stephen Odyek (until May 1987)
80th Brigade	Major John Okello (in 1987)
90th Brigade	
115th Brigade	Captain Mark Lapyem

Meanwhile, a few minor insurgent groups also became active in the Teso region, foremost in the form of the Uganda People's Army (UPA), established in May 1987 under the overall leadership of Peter Otai and military leadership of Captain Francis 'Hitler' Eregu. Organised into four mobile columns, this group was supported by local militias staffed by the recruiting of 10 young men from each village. The UPA accepted women too, and some of these successfully occupied command positions, although most of the militiamen were armed only with bladed weapons – like knives and pangas (machettes).[166]

The Holy Spirit Movement

Another movment – indeed one that was to prove as a deadly competitor to the UPDA, and whose legacy would endure for decades – also appeared in Acholiland in 1986. Designated the Holy Spirit Mobile Forces (HSMF), it was entirely different to any of the other insurgent *organisations* ever active in Uganda. One of its numerous peculiarities was that it was almost single-handedly established by a young woman, Alice Lauma. Born in 1956 near Gulu, in a relatively poor neighbourhood, Lauma completed primary education before conducting a normal life, marked by several break-ups with her successive companions. On 25 May 1985, she claimed to have been possessed by Lakwena, a particularly powerful spirit of Italian origin. Benefitting from the power of this spirit that she said used her as a medium, she began a new career as a healer in Opit, until 6 August 1986, when she said Lakwena ordered her to lead a war against the government in Kampala as well as against witchcraft. Lauma thus established the HSMF as a messianic-style movement, initially recruiting around 80 ex-UNLA and ex-UPDA soldiers who found her mix of local animistic and Christian concepts particularly attractive.[167] Lauma insisted that the leadership of her movement was actually composed of a small number of spirits which communicated with her followers through her as a medium. In this fashion, she created an *organisation* that was highly centralised and operated as a single body, but had a highly unconventional ideological fabric that made it well-structured and allowed it to receive support and attract recruits even when operating outside Acholiland.The HSMF launched its first attack on Gulu on 19 October 1986, when it suffered extensive losses and was forced to withdraw. By November, it had reached the Kitgum area, where it attracted additional former soldiers and even began receiving the support of troops of 70 Brigade UPDA, already operating in the area.[168] In January 1987, the group established a Frontline Co-ordination Team and several War Mobilisation Committees, responsible for mobilising the population and obtaining support. Although by that time the number of the movement's members had increased to between 7,000 and 10,000, its basic *organisation* never varied: composed of combat companies A, B and C, and the HQ company. Each of the companies included between three and 30 platoons of between 50 and 80 men each, divided into three sections. Therefore, a HSMF company could have included as many as 2,400 combatants.[169]The HQ Company was divided into various 'offices', which provided all the support functions of a military service, including Intelligence and Signals, but also Production, Women and Children. The HQ Company also included the Operations Office, composed solely of battle-hardened veterans who acted as shock troops and military police. All members of the HSMF were subjected to draconian discipline and had to follow a strictly-enforced Code of Conduct which included 20 points: the 'Holy Spirit Safety Precautions'. While some of the points in question – like having no more and no less than two testicles, or smoking cigarettes – were rather unusual, others were very similar to the NRA's Code of Conduct. Sexual intercourse between members, killing prisoners or looting civilian property were all strictly prohibited, while all combatants were prohibited from carrying weapons: these were kept by the Armoury office and issued only before an operation.[170]

A group of UPDA insurgents preparing for an attack on NRA positions in the Namokora area. Note the anti-tank rifle grenade (probably of Yugoslav origin) attached to the AK-47 carried by the insurgent to the left. (Fausto Biloslavo)

UPDA insurgents armed with an RPG-7 (left) and a PKT machine gun in 1987. They generally proved no match for the fanaticism of the Holy Spirit Movement, nor the well-disciplined NRA. (Fausto Biloslavo)

The HSMF's military tactics were de-facto dictated by its belief system. Its standard practice was to draw about 250 fighters from each of the operational companies to form a 750-strong assault party. Selected fighters were then issued arms and submitted to various rites which were supposed to protect them from enemy weapons – but also forbid them to take cover. Instead, they were expected to advance bare-chested. Immediately before the start of an attack, they would form a line, sing religious songs for at least 10 minutes and then advance on enemy positions, firing a pre-ordained number of shots before retreating. HSMF combatants were even forbidden to aim while firing because they were not supposed to choose which enemy deserved to die: it was up to the spirits to guide their bullets and strike the 'sinful' among the enemy ranks.Initially, these tactics gave the HSMF several victories; because many of its opponents shared its beliefs, they would panic, thinking the insurgents were invincible. However, whenever confronted by steady and disciplined troops, the Holy Spirit Movement invariably suffered dreadful casualties. Lauma's explanation about such cases was as simple and strange as her order for HSMF fighters not to aim when firing: those who were killed or wounded in battle had been struck by enemy fire because they failed to follow the HSMF's Safety Precautions and therefore compromised the efficiency of the rituals. Unsurprisingly, the fact that the movement took some particularly heavy casualties, combined with all recruitment being on a voluntary basis, eventually forced it to evolve its tactics towards much more conventional practices. Its combatants were eventually authorised to aim when firing and lay ambushes. Indeed, the HSMF became particularly well-versed in setting up ambushes, usually deploying five parties for this purpose: one for early warning, another to block the enemy retreat, the 'killing group' equipped with best weapons, and two flanking groups responsible for protection of the entire force from unforeseen enemy movements.[171]

Lauma's Crusade

After recovering from defeat at Gulu in October 1986, the HSMF returned to attack the NRA post at Corner Kilak – an important crossroads on the Lira–Kitgum Road on 22 November of the same year. Unsurprisingly, it was repulsed and four days later the Army launched a major counter-attack on Lauma's main camp situated nearby. To the surprise of the NRA's commanders, this time its unit was forced to withdraw in complete chaos – and this after only 10 minutes of battle in which it suffered 25 casualities and left behind of arms and ammunition.[172]

The unexpected victory made Lauma famous and prompted several UPDA units active in the same area to join her movement. The HSMF thus deployed 750 of its combatants (armed with 450 firearms) for an attack on NRA positions near Pajule, a market town near the Lira–Kitgum road, on 25 December 1986. Surprisingly, it routed the defenders.On 1 January 1987, Lauma's movement launched its second attempt against Corner Kilak, but this time its 250 combatans suffered heavy casualties, not only during the assault, but especially in the course of the subsequent counter-attack by the NRA unit commanded by Major Sande. Lauma then went to the battlefield with most of the HSMF fighters and prepared the next attack, starting the biggest battle in northern Uganda so far. The first wave of this offensive – once again including 750 fighters – was launched on the morning of 14 January. Sande's troops defeated the insurgents in a fight that lasted an hour and a half. However, they were subsequently taken by surprise when insurgents attacked again during the afternoon, and forced to beat a hasty retreat. Although suffering extensive casualties at Corner Kilak, the HSMF maintained its strength at about 7,000 during this period.[173]Having heard about the loss of Corner Kilak, Major-Genaral Fred Rwigyema – the NRA's second in command, then stationed in Gulu – ordered the Mobile Brigade from Lira and several other units to mount a massive counter-attack on the HSMF. This began on 18 January and was supported by field artillery. Facing insurgents who lined up as usual, the battle-hardened NRA troops manoeuvred around their flanks. The result of this 'battle' was literally a slaughter: over 350 HSMF were killed, with 976 firearms and 33 RPG-7 launchers captured. Nevertheless, the NRA also admitted to having suffered as many as 97 casualties.[174]

Withdrawing towards Pader Kilak, the HSMF was back fighting again two weeks later, launching two large-scale attacks on NRA positions at Puranga on 2 and 16 February, and eventually overrunning them with three successive waves of 450 combatants each.[175] Emboldened, the insurgents then penetrated the Lira District, attracting around 1,500 new recruits despite the presence of the UPA in the area. However, their repeated attempts to capture Lira were all repulsed, and the movement eventually decided to return to Opti in late April 1987.Lauma now opened negotiations with the UPDA and UPA, intending to unite their forces in the struggle against the government, but all such attempts failed because the latter two groups refused to put themselves under the overall command of the HSMF. On the contrary, the failure of negotiations resulted in a bitter rivalry between the Holy Spirit Movement and the Ugandan People's Democratic Army, as the two groups were in competition over the meagre resources of an impoverished population. When the UPDA began to harass isolated HSMF members, Lauma reacted by launching an assault on the HQ of 70 Brigade, and then an even larger enterprise – Operation Coy – against 50 Brigade UPDA on 28 June 1987. Both 'Democrat' units were scattered into swamps around Kitugm and Gulu, and those who were captured were given the choice of either joining the HSMF or being executed on the spot.[176]

The rivalry between insurgents was exploited by the NRA to launch an attack on Lauma's HQ in Opit on 29 June. Taken by surprise, B Company HSMF withdrew instead of reinforcing the hastily-organised counter-attack of A and C Companies, and after only an hour of fighting the Movement abandoned its shrine and fled about 25km (15 miles) towards the east. On 4 July, it attempted to recapture its shrine, but this attack was easily beaten back by the NRA.In late July, the Movement marched into Soroti District, opening negotiations with UPA units which were besieging the town of Soriti. The talks soon degenerated into an open fire-fight and Lauma's combatants killed five UPA officers. The HSMF then continued into Mbale District, but was ambushed by the NRA and mauled on 4 September. Subsequently, the NRA's COIN tactics of combining relatively static zonal detachments and mobile intervention forces proved highly effective in curbing the Movement's advance, then local villages generally supportive of Musveni's government went as far as to track and kill isolated HSMF combatants. Nevertheless, on 7 September, the insurgents gained a minor victory when they ambushed a pursuing NRA battalion, killing 12 soldiers and capturing 24 firearms.[177]

A grim scene from the battlefield at Corner Kilak, with NRA troops beginning to collect the bodies of killed insurgents on 18 January 1987. (Fausto Biloslavo)

Defeat of the HSMF

Lauma's Movement continued operating in the Tororo District for the rest of September, but on the 30th of that month the NRA successfully encircled it and subjected the HQ Company to intensive mortar-fire. The HSMF broke out during 1 October, but only after suffering nearly 35 percent casualties, including more than 500 deserters. After this catastrophe, the cohesion of the Movement greatly dimished and Lauma's authority began to fade.[178] Undaunted, she ordered a new advance along the Tororo–Iganga road towards Jinja on 16 October. Entering the former Kingdom of Busoga, the insurgents found themselves facing an extremely hostile population, and found it ever more difficult to find food. Indeed, locals began reporting their positions to the NRA by beating drums and other means.Ignoring Iganga, on 25 October the HSMF attacked the Magamaga barracks about 18km (10 miles) outside Jinja, but this assault turned into a disaster. The NRA allowed the insurgents to enter the base perimeter before opening a hail of fire from machine guns from short range, killing at least 100 and capturing 60.[179] Only three days later, the last cohesive group was surrounded by the Army and scattered, leaving Lauma with no choice but to flee to Kenya with a few of her most trusted followers. Without its charismatic leader, the Holy Spirit Movement was finished.

Apart from the 'human wave' style of tactics, the major reason for the massive casualties of the HSMF during the Battle of Corner Kilak was that the previous night they ran a spiritual 'party', in the course of which 'holy oil' was spilled over their bodies to make them 'immortal'. Their assault on NRA positions protected by heavy machine guns and anti-aircraft cannons firing anti-personnel ammunition resulted in a catastrophe. (Fausto Biloslavo)

The End of UPDA and UPA

By late 1987, the civil war in Uganda was essentially a stalemate. The increased presence of the NRA in Acholiland, but mainly the devastating blows it received from the HSMF, left the UPDA in a badly weakened position and short of supplies. The insurgents were still largely free to roam the countryside but the government re-settled 33,000 internally displaced persons into protected camps around Gulu, cutting them off from the insurgency. Furthermore, the NRA offered a partial amnesty for all ex-UNLA soldiers. Despite deep mistrust, more than 1,000 insurgents were enticed into abandoning the armed struggle in December 1987 alone.[180] Unsurprisingly, the UPDA leadership offered negotiations and – following preliminary contacts – formal peace talks were held between Salim Saleh and John Angelo Okello in Gulu, in March 1988, although the insurgent political wing was excluded. The talks ended in a ceasefire agreement and the government's promise to provide cash rations for UPDA units. A formal peace agreement was signed on 3 June 1988: it included the release of prisoners held by the government and integration of UPDA officers and other ranks into the NRA – as far as they desired to join.The conflict between the NRA and the UPA in Teso continued and even intensified, nevertheless, as both parties began to make use of torture, rape and murder of civilians suspected of supporting the other side. The Iteso people thus found themselves between the hammer of the government and anvil of the insurgents, while additionally facing armed bandits.[181]The UPA did not launch any major attacks, but operated primilarly hit-and-run tactics. On 12 March 1988, it derailed a train near Nagongera, overcame the soldiers protecting it and ransacked the passengers. The NRA sought to destroy insurgent camps while implementing the policy of forced relocation of around 120,000 villagers into protected camps to create fire-free zones. Reports of atrocities

A group of insurgents of the United Holy Salvation Army in the early 1990s. Although wearing military fatigues and relatively well-armed, very few of them had any military background, and even less any military training. (Wikimedia commons)

against civilians began to grow in number. On 11 July 1989, Chris Bunyenyzi, CO 106th Battalion NRA – a Tutsi-Rwandan raised in exile in Uganda – locked 120 suspected UPA sympathisers into a rail wagon at the Okungolo railway station and left them inside for the entire day: 69 died from thirst, heat and lack of breathing space. Worse was to follow as most of the government-controlled camps lacked the necessary infra-structure to support thousands of people, and an estimated average of 15 people died each day in different camps as a result of harsh living conditions and endemic outbreaks of cholera and dysentery between 1987 and 1992.[182]Only then did the NRA start to reduce its presence in the district and allow civilians to return to their villages. Finding itself deprived of local and outside support, without a connection to the population to feed its troops, the UPA was progressively weakened. By 1991, most of its cadre quit the struggle, enticed by Kampala's amnesty. The last few UPA groups surrendered in 1995.

Emergence of the Lord Resistance Army

In early 1986, a certain Joseph Kony – born in 1961 in Odek (Gulu District), the son of a former soldier of the King's African Rifles – declared to have been possessed by a spirit named Juma Oris and became a traditional healer in the fashion of Alice Luma. During March 1986, Kony began to preach and gathered a small group of followers. At some point, he met Alice Lauma in Opit and temporarily allied himself with the then fast-growing HSMF, but was soon humiliated by her and left to become a fierce rival. Although rallying a number of former HSMF-combatants, Kony's group rather resembled an armed gang until the defeat of Lauma's Movement in October 1987, when it was reinforced by numerous survivors of the fighting around Jinja. Kony then established the United Holy Salvation Army and entered into a temporary alliance with the UPDA, but betrayed the latter while preparing a joint attack on Gulu later the same year.On 19 January 1988, Kony's Salvation Army attacked 115 Brigade UPDA and managed to convice most of its fighters – including the CO, Captain Mark Lapyem – to switch sides. Lapyem subsequently became one of Kony's closest aides and advisers, and it was probably his advice that led to the first major success of the *organisation* – an attack on the NRA's position near Bibia, in late April 1988, in the course of which a 1,000-strong force killed 34 government troops while losing 36 of their own.[183]

The peace treaty of June 1988 proved a two-fold benediction for Kony. On one side, it removed the UPDA rival; on the other, some of the insurgents decided to continue their struggle against Kampala and about 39 of them – led by Brig Odong Latek – rallied to the Salvation Army, meanwhile re-organised as the People's Democratic Christian Army (UPDCA). Furthermore, Kony eliminated another rival when capturing Severino Lukoya – Lauma's father – in August 1988. Although only marginally involved in the HSMF venture, the latter attempted to reconstitute it, but experienced an early defeat during an assault on Kitgum in May 1989.[184]Although its early success attracted a number of willing volunteers, the UPDCA quickly experienced difficulties in recruiting the Acholi population; the latter grew war-wary over its devastated homeland. Hence, as early as April 1988, the *organisation* began abducting children and kidnapping adults and forcefully enlisting them, although still on a limited scale compared to what was to follow during the next decade. The movement's resort to abduction grew only over time, resulting in thousands of kidnapped villagers between 1989 and 1991.[185]While Latek's career with the UPDCA was quite brief (he was killed in an NRA ambush in 1989), the influence of the former UPDA military commander was sufficient to convince Kony to drastically change his military tactics. He adapted the classic guerrilla approach to warfare, operating in small groups which conducted hit-and-run attacks instead of the HSMF's massive assaults. Therefore, the UPDCA evolved into a hybrid of the HSMF and UPDA, and became far more elusive – greatly improving its long-term survival prospects in return.

At the top of Kony's *organisation* was a type of high command named Trinity, which controlled a total of four 'divisions' named Condum, Stockry, Gilver and Prinini, each divided into three sections named Father, Son and Holy Ghost. The movement had a 'special' force called the Special Mobile Brigade – possibly designated the Trinklee or Control Altar at some point. Most female fighters were organised into the Mary Company. Despite their designations, it is doubtful if any of these groups ever had more than a few hundred combatants.[186]

Operation North

After several years which saw successive waves of violence in Acholiland, and probably enticed by the World Bank which conditioned the delivery of financial help to develop the north of the country, Kampala decided to launch an all-out offensive and destroy the UPDCA. Deploying the mass of its mobile units under the command of Major-Genaral David Tinyefuza (the NRM's Minister of Defence), the NRA cut off the districts of Apac, Gulu, Lira and Kitgum from the outside world in early April 1991, and then launched a search-and-destroy operation.[187] Although organising a local militia to help his troop track insurgents, Tinyefuza refused to arm and fund this group. The militiamen were therefore forced to arm themselves with bows and spears, and became known as 'Arrow Groups'. Worse still, reports about extensive human rights violations – including summary executions, abductions, torture and rape – were not long in coming. Between 14 and 18 April, the 22nd Battalion NRA (CO Major Reuben Ikondere) detained hundreds of villagers in the Burcoro Primary School, repeatedly gang raped men and women and murdered seven suspected UPDCA sympathisers.[188]The combination of a massive Army presence and operations of Arrow Groups devastated the insurgency, although the exact extent of its losses remains unknown. Betty Bigombe, the NRM's Minister for the Pacification of the North, announced that 3,000 UPDCA were 'eliminated' in Kitgum District in May 1991 alone, but such estimates usually reflected the NRA's overconfidence. Indeed, the military quickly proclaimed this operation a victory and ended it in July, although Tinyefuza admitted that it would be left to Arrow Groups to finish Kony's movement without any NRA support. This decision proved a major blunder when, although suffering extensive losses, Kony and his followers – meanwhile calling themselves the Lord's Resistance Army (LRA) – remained strong enough to launch a big campaign of reprisals against the militiamen and the communities supporting them, usually cutting limbs of their victims to dissuade others from betraying the movement. Unsurprisingly, the ill-equipped Arrow Groups were nearly annihiliated by early 1992.[189]

Either relenting from the blows it received during Operation North, or unable to maintain a high level of activities for long, in mid-1993 the LRA agreed to enter into negotiations with the government. The first meeting between Bigombe, Colonel Adam Wasswa (CO 4th Division) and LRA middle-ranking officers took place in mid-1993, in Gulu. On 11 January 1994, Bigombe met Kony, and the talks were encouraging in so far that a ceasefire was agreed. However, although the minister enjoyed the support of Wasswa and Museveni, negotiations proved unpopular within the NRM and the entire process was derailed during the third meeting, on 24 January 1994. Instead, Museveni imposed an ultimatum on all insurgents to surrender within six days, on 6 February, causing the LRA to withdrew from the talks and resume the war.[190]

It was around this point that the nature and dynamics of the civil war in Uganda changed completely and this conflict became a part of a large power play in central Africa. Namely, during the early 1990s, the NRM not only entered into co-operation with the Sudanese People's Liberation Army in southern Sudan, but also the USA. Museveni, meanwhile, established particularly close ties to Rwanda – since 1994 ruled by a group of Rwandan Tutsi exiles who grew up in Uganda and occupied several leading positions within the NRA before defecting to start an insurgency in their own country.[191] However, that was an entirely different story, to be told in a future volume of this series.

(Endnotes)

1. Uganda; Library of Congress Country Studies, citing Henry Morton Stanley's report from 1875.
2. Dupuy et al, p. 270
3. Omara-Otunni, pp. 51, 66
4. Omara-Otunni, pp. 58–67; the reason for Israeli interest in co-operating with Uganda was to overcome its isolation in the Middle East through gaining political influence in Africa.
5. Omara-Otunni, pp. 71–79
6. The 12 Shermans delivered by Israel in 1969 included a few examples with early suspension and others with HVSS-suspension and wider tracks. All were armed with the 76mm calibre M1 gun.
7. Dupuy et al, p. 270; Omara-Otunni, pp. 81–86
8. Cooper et al, African MiGs, Volume 2, p. 177. The first Israeli-trained Ugandan pilots soloed in time to take part in the fly-past over Kampala during Independence Day celebrations in 1964. Thanks to the intensive work of Israeli instructors, the number of qualified Ugandan pilots increased significantly over the following years.
9. Czechoslovak documentation clearly states that this contract came into being with the help of bribes for the Ugandan MoD Felix Onamo, who was promised 3–4 percent of the total value of the contract. The same documentation further indicated that the CoS Ugandan Army, Opoleto, was bribed too. Although not directly mentioning this, corresponding reports cited Opoleto's 'very positive attitude to the financial values'.
10. Cooper et al, African MiGs, Volume 2, pp. 177–78
11. Obviously, this extension of the project caused cost overruns and had a negative impact on the morale of Ugandans. Czechoslovaks developed some negative feelings too: modifications to the contract were not very favourable for them, and repeated reassessment of the training eventually caused a flying accident.
12. Nine Ugandans were trained as aircraft technicians in Czechoslovakia, four as technicians for electric equipment and instruments, two as technicians for radio equipment and two as technicians for aircraft armament: 15 of them qualified with notes 'very good' or 'excellent', and three with 'good'.
13. Hlado was a highly-experienced pilot, a graduate of the Military

Academy in Hranice and Prostejov and test pilot for the Avia Company in the late 1930s. In 1942, he joined the RAF in the UK and flew Supermarine Spitfires for the rest of the Second World War, becoming CO Czechoslovak Fighter Wing. After returning to Czechoslovakia, he survived purges and repression after the Communist coup of 1948, and subsequently served as senior officer for training of foreign personnel. Prior to being sent to Uganda, he served for two years as a military adviser to Indonesia. He was posthumously promoted to Major-General on 1 January 1991.

14. 'Revealed: How Israel Helped Amin to Take Power', *The Independent*, 17 August 2003; notable is that the head of the Israeli Defence Force mission in Uganda of the late 1960s was Colonel Bar-Lev, who later became famous for constructing the Bar-Lev Line along the Suez Canal (see Omara-Otunni, p. 98).
15. Omara-Otunni, p. 107; Amin's bizarre and often ad hoc fashion of promoting officers can best be seen in examples such as the following:Sergeant-Major Mustafa Adrisi: although illiterate, rose quickly to the rank of major-general, and held the posts of the Chief of Staff, Minister of Defence and Vice-President of Uganda;Yakobo Abiriga: serving as a lieutenant in 1971, was promoted immediately after the coup to lieutenant-colonel and appointed the CO of Mubende Battalion;
16. Elly Hassan Hassan Drony (from the same Kakwa ethnic group as Amin): only a sergeant in 1968, was advanced in rank by Amin up to colonel in 1974. The mess Amin created within the UA's chain of command was further complicated by the fact that anybody enjoying direct connection to the top of the state and military had more influence and the last word when issuing commands, even if a junior officer by rank. Omara-Otunni, p. 129
17. This chapter is largely based on Wulf Petermann, 'Die Flieger des Julius Nyerere', *Fliegerrevue Extra*, Vol. 26 (September 2009); in turn, that article was based on interviews with one of the Chinese advisers involved in Tanzania in the 1970s, as well as CIA documentation released in response to a FOIA inquiry. Additional sources included Pollack, *Arabs at War*, and the blog by Idi Amin Awongo Alemi Dada, the son of the then President of Uganda, in 2009 available at: www.idiamindada.com/A_Daring_Rescue.html
18. Dupuy et al, p. 263
19. Dupuy, p. 264
20. Ibid, p. 263
21. Henry Lubega, 'How my Operation in Tanzania turned Deadly', *The Citizen* (3 June 2014). Badly injured, Kisuula was carried back to Uganda by his 'recruits' and then evacuated by helicopter to Masaka hospital. He recovered after surgery by a Norwegian doctor, and returned to service only three weeks later.
22. Omara-Otunni, p. 122
23. Avirgan et al, p. 34
24. Museveni, pp. 1–23, 54–56
25. Avirgan et al, pp. 35–36; Museveni, p. 59
26. Cooper et al, *African MiGs, Vol. 2*, p. 185
27. Flintham, p. 151; Museveni, p. 62
28. Museveni, p. 65
29. Museveni, p. 66. By comparison, Omara-Otunni (p. 120) reported a six-hour long battle and that this group lost over 100 KIA before it was forced to withdraw.
30. Museveni, p. 69. By comparison, Omara-Otunni (p. 120) reported that this convoy was stopped near Kiziba by a, 'much larger UA force supported by tanks and APCs, and lost about 20 KIA in a battle before retreating into Tanzania'.
31. Flintham, p. 151
32. For details on Libyan orders for Mirages from France, and their service in the period 1970–1974, see Cooper et al, *Arab MiGs, Volumes 4, 5, and 6* and accompanying Volume 18 from Africa@War series, *Libyan Air Wars, Part 1.*
33. Ibid, p. 151; Museveni, p. 70; Omara-Otunni, p. 120. Notable is that Flintham cited reports according to which it is possible that the LAAF deployed several of its Dassault Mirage 5D fighter-bombers to Entebbe IAP, and that these flew attacks on Bakuba and Mwanza. Such reports remain unconfirmed until now.
34. Avirgan et al, p. 36; Museveni, p.71
35. As US diplomatic cables from the 1973–1976 period reveal, during the folowing years the USA established military links with Kenya with the aim of helping this country defend itself against perceived threats of invasion from Uganda. One of the results of this co-operation was the delivery of Northrop F-5E Tiger II fighter jets to Nairobi. For details see Kevin Kelley, 'Kenyatta, Kissinger and the Fighter Jets', *The East African* (20 June 2006).
36. Avirgan et al, p. 12
37. Cooper et al, *African MiGs Vol. 2*, p. 179; Omara-Otunni, p. 123. Notable is that while frequently reported in numerous sources, the delivery of 50 PT-76 light tanks to Uganda remains unconfirmed: not only were no photographs of any such vehicles in that country ever taken, but the presence of as many light tanks would have enabled the UA to establish more than only one armoured regiment equipped with tanks. While Omara-Otunni reports deliveries of up to 80 Saladin armoured cars by Libya, their presence was confirmed only by Ruvehururu, but in much smaller numbers (probably in squadron-strength). Finally, delivery of 'seven helicopters' from the Soviet Union cannot be confirmed, while most of the 'Soviet' APCs in question were actually Czechoslovak-built OT-64 SKOTs.
38. Petermann, 'Die Flieger des Julius Nyerere', *Fliegerrevue Extra*, Vol. 26 (September 2009), pp. 72–73
39. Ibid, p. 82; both tables are based on the same source.
40. Based on Wulf Petermann, 'Die Flieger des Julius Nyerere', *Fliegerrevue Extra*, Vol. 26 (September 2009).
41. When studying the history of the Ugandan military under Amin, it must be kept in mind that many details remain obscure. Promotions were issued randomly, usually depending on an officer's connection with Amin. It often happened that a junior officer had more influence than his superiors and the latter would not risk contradicting him.
42. Notably, while Ugandan officials subsequently admitted the destruction of '11 MiGs' during an Israeli attack (see 'Amin Gets New Soviet Jets', *The Lewiston Daily Sun*, 3 January 1977), the Israelis claimed to have destroyed only three MiG-17s on the northern and five MiG-21s on the southern apron of Entebbe IAP.
43. Eyal Ben, 'Special: Entebbe's unsung hero', *Yenetnews*, 3 July 2009
44. Avirgan et al, p. 18. According to Avirgan, despite near-simultaneous tensions with the USA, some links to the West were still maintained. For example, about two dozen Ugandan police pilots and mechanics received a 'refresher' course at the Bell Helicopter Company's school in Fort Worth, USA, while Great Britain sold specialised equipment to the SRB.
45. 'Amin Gets New Soviet Jets', *The Lewiston Daily Sun*, 3 January 1977; *Sarasota Herald Tribune*, 7 March 1977. Local US newspaper *Lakeland Ledger* reported the defection of Ugandan pilot Timothy Lwanga to the USA on 27 April 1977. Lwanga was trained in Czechoslovakia and then the USSR to fly Soviet MiGs. He was then sent to Kenya to serve with Safari Air and Uganda National Airliners before defecting. Following Uganda's military defeat in April 1979, most UAAF pilots found refuge in Libya, where they were integrated into the LAAF, together with several pilots who managed to escape the Tanzanian invasion (for details see 'Uganda Pilots Fly Libya MiGs', *New Vision*, 30 April 2001).
46. Omara-Otunni, pp. 139–40; *Reading Eagle*, 27 May 1978
47. Avigran et al, p. 54
48. Henry Lubega, 'Tanzanians found Amin Men weak – Colonel Kisuule', *Inyenyere News*, 25 May 2014. This and all subsequent quotations from Kisuule are based on the same article.
49. Born into an Ankole family to a father who was conscripted into the British colonial army, Rwehururu joined the UA as a cadet in 1965 and was trained in India. One of the few Acholi officers to remain in the military after Amin's coup of 1971, he was promoted to major in 1974 and assigned to the 5th Mechanised Specialist Reconnaissance Regiment. From 1975 until 1978, he served in the Economic Crime Tribunal under the Minister of Justice, until re-assigned to the military. This and all subsequent quotations by Rwehururu are from his book *Cross to the Gun*, published in 2002.
50. Avigran et al, p. 59
51. Ibid, pp. 37, 51
52. Ibid, p. 59; *Ocala Star Banner*, 31 October 1978
53. Avigran et al, p. 60; *Milwaukee Sentinel*, 1 November 1978
54. Ibid, pp. 61–63
55. Henry Lubega, 'The Untold Story of Kagera War by TZ, Uganda Top Soldiers', *The Citizen*, 15 July 2015; this and all subsequent quotations from Lupembe are based on excerpts from the same article.
56. The man who blew up the Kyuka Bridge was a British engineer brought in from the Kalembe Copper Mine in the Ruwenzori Mountains. His charges dropped only the centre section of 75 metres, without damaging the stanchions: This later enabled Tanzanians to repair this crucial installation relatively quickly.
57. Avigran et al, p. 66. Note that authors of this otherwise excellent book

misidentified the SAMs used as SA-2s; Tanzania never purchased such weapons, and the SAMs in question were almost certainly SA-3s. Furthermore, they cited three MiGs as shot down (other sources cited as many as five): available evidence indicates only the loss of two F-6s and Akiirusha's death.
58. Ibid, p. 68
59. Cooper et al, *African MiGs, Vol. 2*, p. 169
60. Avigran et al, p. 78
61. Museveni, p. 97
62. Henry Lubega, 'Facing naked Ugandan Women on the Frontline', *The Citizen*, 4 June 2014
63. Avigran et al, p. 75
64. Ibid, p. 79
65. Henry Lubega, 'Tanzanians found Amin Men weak – Colonel Kisuule', *Inyenyere News*, 25 May 2014.
66. Avigran et al, p. 69
67. Ibid, p. 70
68. Museveni, p. 98
69. Avigran et al, p. 80
70. *Eugene Register Guard*, 17 February 1979
71. Ibid
72. Avigran et al, p. 82; Museveni, p. 98
73. Avigran et al, p. 83
74. Cooper et al, pp. 170–71
75. In a classic example of their inability to provoke an uprising against Amin, about 200 insurgents loyal to Obote and grouped inside Kenya launched an attempt to capture Tororo, in eastern Uganda, on 2 March 1979. Their sympathisers inside the military barracks of Tororo opened this operation by shooting at Amin loyalists, and the insurgents – dressed in old UA uniforms – then stormed the garrison. Amin forces fled and the armoury was captured quickly. However, the guerrillas then found they could not evacuate captured arms and ammunition due to the lack of suitable vehicles. While they attempted to haul away whatever they could carry, loyalist reinforcements from Mubende arrived, supported by UAAF MiGs. Hitting everybody they saw – loyalist soldiers and insurgents alike – they caused them all to flee for the Kenyan border: guerrillas, Amin soldiers, anti-Amin soldiers and civilians. Kenyan authorities (Nairobi took a pro-Amin stance during the Kagera War) waited at the border, arresting anyone they could get their hands upon. Whoever failed to flee was subsequently mopped up by the SRB. For details, see Avigran et al, pp. 87–88; *Toledo Blade*, 3 March 1979; *The Bulletin*, 3 March 1979. According to the latter two sources, the UA was even at this stage able to rush additional reinforcements from Jinja to Tororo with the help of commandeered civilian transport aircraft, while air strikes by UAAF MiGs proved crucial for the defeat of this insurgent operation.
76. Henry Lubega, 'Tanzanians found Amin Men weak – Colonel Kisuule', *Inyenyere News*, 25 May 2014
77. Avigran et al, pp. 90, 93; notable is that – according to the same source – most of the Libyans deployed to Uganda were not regulars from the LAA, but militiamen from the Libyan People's Militia, with little training and experience, which explained why they would run a joint exercise with the Ugandan Army.
78. Ibid, p. 91
79. Ibid, pp. 91–92; according to Avigran and Honey, it being said that Libyans were in Uganda to capture slaves, Tanzanians summarily executed some of them.
80. Ibid, p. 93
81. Museveni, pp. 98–100
82. Faking radio signals from the major Ugandan airport, in one instance Tanzanians caused the crew of a Boeing 707 airliner of the Belgian SABENA company to land at Mwanza airfield. Finding the aircraft empty (it was about to pick up a load of coffee for Djibouti), but lacking the fuel and equipment to launch it from Mwanza again, Tanzanians placed the crew in the best rooms of the New Mwanza Hotel. The next morning, a military transport flew the necessary equipment from Dar es-Salaam and the SABENA plane was sent on its way. For details, see Avigran et al, p. 94.
83. *St Petersburg Times*, 31 March 1979
84. Yoweri Museveni, 'The Qaddafi I know', *Foreign Policy*, 24 March, 2011
85. Avigran et al, p. 120; *Free-Lance Star*, 3 April 1979
86. Avigran et al, pp. 122–23
87. *Sunday Star*, News Section, 2 April 1979; *The Age*, 3 April 1979
88. Avigran et al, pp. 124–25; 'Tanzania Mounts Massive Attack on Ugandan Capital', *The Prescot Courier*, 9 April 1979. Some JWTZ officers joked about the good luck of the 19th Battalion, one sarcastically observing, 'It's incredible. This is like a Chinese war film. You never see any of the good guys getting killed.'
89. Avigran et al, p. 196
90. Museveni, pp. 122–23
91. Although colloquially called the 'Western Nile Front', this *organisation* had no official designation; at best, its members tended to call themselves 'Uganda Army'. The situation changed only once it later split into the UNRF and FUNA. For details see 'Negotiating Peace: Resolution of Conflicts in Uganda's West Nile Region', Refugee Law Project, Working Paper No.12, 1999, p. 1.
92. Rwehururu, pp. 148–49; while designated the 'Western Front' in this book for the reader's easier orientation, the exact designation of the *organisation* in question remains unclear to this today.
93. Ibid, pp. 151–53
94. Kasozi, pp. 168–69, 179
95. Kasozi, pp,161, 167; Kutesa, p. 126
96. Kutesa, pp. 127–29; Cowell, *NYT*, 25 February 1982; Museveni, p. 149
97. Kutesa, p. 147; Museveni, p. 149
98. Rwehururu, pp. 121–23
99. This lack of weapons was to prove a continuous hindrance for the PRA during the following war, forcing its leaders to always carefully balance the amount of weapons and ammunition they could expect to gain in specific operations against the amount they were likely to spend or lose. In turn, this problem encouraged them to train their fighters very carefully, ensuring these would maintain strict fire discipline in combat.
100. Museveni, pp. 121–23
101. Kainerugaba, *Battles of the Ugandan Resistance*, pp. 66–67; Museveni, p. 126
102. Ibid, pp. 127–30, 133
103. Omara-Otunni, p. 151; Alan Cowell, *NYT*, 22 December 1981
104. Newly-established services included not only the Special Force, but also the UPC Youth Wing (a 5,000-strong militia) and the National Security Agency (NASA), which was primarily responsible for preventing coup plotting from within the UNLA (see Omara-Otunni, p. 161).
105. Kasozi, p. 147
106. Kutesa, pp. 128, 135
107. Ibid, p. 24, 26
108. *Reuters*, 13 June 1981; Alan Cowell, *NYT*, 25 February 1982; Turner, p. 212
109. Alan Cowell, *Glasgow Herald*, 15 December 1981; *Corporatewatch.org*, 'Thatcher backed Ugandan crackdown', 29 May 2014
110. Prunier, p. 108; Kutesa, pp. 184, 186, 189
111. Kutesa, p. 155; Timothy Kalyegira, 'What Killed Gen Oyite-Ojok?', *monitor.co.uk*, 25 June 2014
112. Kutesa, p. 68
113. Ibid, p. 65
114. Museveni, p. 137
115. Kutesa, pp. 73, 82
116. Museveni, p. 137; Kutesa, p. 85
117. Museveni, p. 141
118. Prunier, pp. 106–07
119. Ibid, p. 146
120. Clapham, pp. 101–02
121. Museveni, p. 147; Weinstein, p. 145
122. Kutesa, p. 83
123. Museveni (*NRA Code of Conduct*), p. 148; Kainerugaba, p. 121
124. Weinstein, p. 177
125. Sources differ, but by various accounts no less than between 2,000 and 3,000 RCs had been established by 1983, each controlling about 40 households on average (Weinstein, p. 180). Aside from managing their day-to-day life, these committees tried minor offences, arbitrated between classic neighbourhood conflicts and had a significant para-military role because they were responsible for collecting food and supplies for the NRA (Kasfir, p. 272).
126. Weinstein, pp. 219, 222, 225
127. Ibid, pp. 222, 225, 371; *Military Review*, November–December 2008, p. 7. Notable is that NRA insurgents were not allowed to execute any of their prisoners, no matter what the circumstances.
128. Clapham, p. 125; Kinzer, p. 47
129. Weinstein, pp. 140, 144
130. Museveni, p. 147
131. Kutesa, pp. 115–16, 128, 142. One of the major problems with new recruits was that many believed in magic and had to be taught not to fear the supposedly 'superior amulets' protecting the UNLA's northerners.

Another widespread prejudice was about the lethality of firearms: many Ugandans believed that the sounds emitted by firearms could also cause injuries, and that artillery shells were able to track their targets. In most cases, the best 'cure' was to let the fighters see with their own eyes that such beliefs were wrong. On the other hand, as these beliefs were shared by the enemy ranks, they enabled the NRA fighters to gain tremendous prestige by defeating 'especially powerful weapons'. One classic example of such tactics resulted in the capture of a M4A1 Sherman tank, refurbished by the UNLA and pressed into service, at an unknown date in 1981. The tank in question was immobilised due to mechanical failure and then knocked out by an RPG-7 round. Its crew was so impressed by 'such a feat' that it immediately opted to join the NRA.

132. Museveni, pp. 148–51
133. Museveni, pp. 141–42; according to Museveni, the lion's share of this shipment went to the UFM, while the NRA received only 96 rifles, five machine guns and eight RPG-7s.
134. Kasozi, p. 172; Museveni, p. 150; Kutesa, pp. 133, 139–40; Turner, p. 212; Weinstein, p. 256
135. Kainerugaba, p. 103; Museveni, p. 153; Kutesa, p. 151
136. Museveni, p. 150; Kutesa, p. 154
137. Particularly useful were good relations with Banyankole cattle-herders, who provided 21,000 cattle in exchange for promises to be paid after victory. Herds of cattle proved easier to defend because of their mobility, although also easier to detect by UNLA helicopters. For details, see Museveni, pp. 155–60.
138. Kainerugaba, pp. 99–100; Museveni, p. 159; Kutesa, pp. 181–83; the entire NRA possessed only some 1,300 rifles before this operation.
139. Kainerugaba, p. 117; Kutesa p. 191
140. John Muto-Ono p'Lajur, 'My Last Days in Luweero With Lieutenant-Colonel Ogole, RIP', *acholitimes.com*, 23 May 2014; Kainerugaba, p. 128
141. Museveni, p. 160; Kutesa, p. 186
142. Kainerugaba, pp. 128–33
143. Kainerugaba, p. 135; Museveni, p. 166; Omara-Otunnu, pp. 162–65; Kutesa, pp. 204–07
144. Kainerugaba, p. 142; Omara-Otunnu, pp. 168–86; Kutesa, pp. 212–15; Weinstein, pp. 268–69
145. Kainerugaba, p. 145; Kutesa, pp. 215–17, 235
146. Joshua Kato, 'Katonga Bridge, the Jewel of the Liberation', *newvision.co.ug*, 23 January 2014;& Kutesa, pp. 221–23
147. Kainerugaba, p. 145; Kutesa, p.232
148. Kainerugaba, p. 149; Museveni, p.169
149. Kainerugaba, pp. 157–60, Museveni, p. 166; Kutesa, p. 210. Except for armament captured in Mbarara and Masaka, the NRA equipped its new units with arms provided by Tanzania (which sent 14 truckloads of firearms and ammunition) and Libya (which used Ilyushin Il-76 transports to airdrop a shipment of 800 firearms and 800,000 rounds of ammunition to the Ngoma area). Interestingly, the latter included a sizeable number of Israeli-made Uzi machine guns, which NRA fighters found 'vastly inferior' to Soviet-made AKM rifles.
150. Kainerugaba, pp. 160–63; Museveni, pp. 160–68
151. Person who used to live in Kampala in1986, interview provided on condition of anonymity, March 2013.
152. Kainerugaba, pp. 160–78; Museveni, pp. 169–70; Kutesa, pp. 239–40
153. Kainerugaba, pp. 163–78; Museveni, pp. 169–71; Kutesa, pp. 238–44
154. Behrend, p. 24; Kutesa, pp. 250–51; Museveni, pp. 172–73
155. Biloslavo; Cooper, *Great Lakes Holocaust*, pp. 22–24
156. Biloslavo; Castlelein, p. 34; Cooper, *Great Lakes Holocaust*, p. 23; Ugandan Ministry of Defence website; Faustin Mugabe, 'Was Rwygema assassinated?' *The Path of a Genocide & Daily Monitor*, 1 October 2014
157. Mondo, p. 91
158. John et al, p. 10; Cooper, *Great Lakes Holocaust*, p. 22
159. Gersony, pp. 6, 13
160. Behrend, p. 24; Castelein, p. 22; Documentation of Teso Women, p. 3
161. Biloslavo; Gersony, p. 13; Nyeko et al, p. 22
162. Branch, p. 10; Museveni, p. 177
163. JRP/FN XIX, pp. 22–25; the 35th Battalion was later disbanded as a consequence of this atrocity; nevertheless, the unit established and deployed in its place apparently showed similar behaviour towards local civilians.
164. *Let my People Go*, p. 34
165. Notable is that the 'brigades' and 'divisions' in question were actually mere companies, hardly any of them stronger than 200–300.
166. Behrend, p. 88; Documentation of Teso Women, pp. 1–3, 56
167. Behrend, pp. 25, 73, 131–32
168. Ibid, p. 25; about 150 UPDA combatants were granted permission to join the HSM.
169. Ibid, pp. 69–70
170. Ibid, pp. 44–55
171. Ibid, pp. 57–61, 151
172. Behrend, pp. 79–80; Bilsolavo
173. Ibid, pp. 80–81; Faustin Mugabe, 'The Book Rwigyema Never Wrote', *Daily Monitor*, 6 October 2013; Museveni, p. 178
174. Biloslavo, 'Rebels in Uganda', *JDW* Vol. 7/No. 23 13 June 1987
175. Behrend, p. 82
176. Ibid, pp. 86–98
177. Behrend, p. 89; Museveni, p. 178
178. Behrend, p. 90; Philip Williams, *LA-Times*, 22 November 1987
179. Behrend, p. 92; 'Report: Troops kill 100 Rebels in Battle at Army Base', *Associated Press*, 26 October 1987
180. Behrend, p. 172; Branch, p. 15; Lamwaka, p.30
181. Documentation of Teso Women, pp. 6, 17
182. De Berry, pp. 71–72; JRP/FN XII, pp. 11–12; Documentation of Teso Women, p. 62
183. Behrend, pp. 161, 178
184. Oloya, pp. 158–62; Severino Lukoya managed to escape from the UPDCA, but was caught and jailed again in August of the same year – this time by the NRA.
185. Behrend, pp. 183–88; Nyeko et al, p. 18; Mutaizibwa, 'The Roots of War: How Alice Lakwena gave way to Joseph Kony', *observer.ul*, 11 August 2011; the early UPDCA was far more lenient with its combatants than the HSM in punishing sex-related infractions: instead, it began hijacking girls to satisfy the sexual desires of its members.
186. Behrend, pp. 183–85; Castelein, p. 33
187. Branch, p. 16;& *Let my People Go*, p. 35
188. Castelein, p. 38; JRP/FN XVII, pp. 5–7, 22, 30
189. Behrend, p. 187; Branch, pp. 16–17; *Let my People Go*, p. 35
190. Branch, p. 18
191. Cooper, *Great Lakes Holocaust*, pp. 22–24; Gersony, p. 78; Okello, p. 23

SELECTED BIBLIOGRAPHY

Acker, F. Van, 'Uganda and the Lord's Resistance Army: The New Order No One Ordered', *Affrican Affairs* Vol. 103, Issue 412, (2004).

Adelman, Howard & Suhrke, Astri (eds) *The Path of a Genocide: The Rwandan Crisis from Uganda to Zaire* (New Brunswick: Transaction Publishers, 2000). ISBN: 978-0765807687

Avirgan, T. & Honey, M., *War in Uganda: The Legacy of Idi Amin* (Dar es-Salaam: Tanzania Publishing House, 1983). ISBN: 9976-1-0056-6

Ball, R., *Camouflage & Markings No.3: The Israeli Air Force, Part One, 1948 to 1967* (Luton: Guideline Publications/Scale Aircraft Monographs, 2001). ISBN: 0-9539040-1-6

Behrend, H. , *Alice Lakwena & the Holy Spirits: War in Northern Uganda, 1985–1997* (Martlesham, Suffolk: James Currey Ltd, 1999). ISBN: 978-0821413111

Berry, J. de, *Life after Loss: An Anthropoligical Study of Post-War Recovery, Teso, East Uganda, with special Reference to Young People* (Ph.D thesis, London School of Economics and Political Science, 2000).

Biloslavlo, F., 'Rebels of Uganda', *Jane's Defence Weekly*, Vol. 7, Number 23, 13 (June 1987).

Branch, A., 'Neither Peace nor Justice: Political Violence and the Peasantry in Northern Uganda, 1986–1998', *African Studies Quarterly*, Vol. 8, Issue 2 (2005).

Brent, Winston, *African Air Forces* (Nelspruit, South Africa: Freeworld Publications, 1999).

Bugakov, I. S., Ivanov, B. V., Kartashev, V. B., Lavrentev, A. P., Ligav, V. A. & PASHKO, V. A., *Kazan Helicopters: Flight Goes On* (Russia: Vertolet Publisher and Kazan Helicopters, 2001).

Castelein, K. J., *Counter-Insurgency in the Greater North of Uganda: Understanding the Auxiliary Forces* (Utrecht: Univeriteit Utrecht, 2008).

Cooper, T., *Great Lakes Holocaust: First Congo War, 1996–1997* (Solihull: Helion & Co, 2013; Africa@War Volume 13). ISBN: 978-1909384651

Cooper, T., *Great Lakes Conflagration: Second Congo War, 1998–2003* (Solihull: Helion & Co, 2013; Africa@War Volume 14). ISBN: 978-1-909384-66-8

Cooper, T., Bishop, F. & HUBERS, A., 'Bombed By Blinders: Tupolev Tu-22s in Action', *Air Enthusiast* magazine, Vol. 116 (March/April 2005).

Cooper, T., Canyon, C. & Grandolini, A., 'Libyens Luftwaffe – von König Idris bis Oberst Gaddafi', *Fliegerrevue Extra* magazine, Vol. 29, (June 2010).
Cooper, T. & Weinert, P., with Hinz, F. & Lepko, M., *African MiGs, MiGs and Sukhois in Service in Sub-Saharan Africa, Volume 1: Angola to Ivory Coast* (Houston: Harpia Publishing LLC, 2010). ISBN 978-0-9825539-5-4
Cooper, T. & Weinert, P., with Hinz, F. & Lepko, M., *African MiGs, MiGs and Sukhois in Service in Sub-Saharan Africa, Volume 2: Madagascar to Zimbabwe* (Houston: Harpia Publishing LLC, 2011). ISBN 978-0-9825539-5
Dupuy, T. N. (Colonel, US Army, ret.), and Blanchard W. (Colonel, US Army, ret.) *The Almanac of World Military Power* (New York: Dunn Loring/ London, T. N. Dupuy Associates/Arthur Barker Ltd, 1972).
ISBN: 0-213-16418-3
Fegley, R., 'Local Needs and Agency Conflict: A Case Study of Kajo Keji County, Sudan', *African Studies Quarterly*, Vol. 11, Issue 1 (2009).
Flintham, V., *Air Wars and Aircraft: a Detailed Record of Air Combat 1945 to the Present* (London: Arms and Armour Press, 1989).
ISBN: 0-85368-779-X
Gersony, R., *The Anguish of Northern Uganda: Results of a Field-Based Assessment of the Civil Conflict in Northern Uganda* (Kampala: USAID Mission, Kampala, 1997).
John, J. Di & Putzel, J., *Institutional Change for Growth and Poverty Reduction in Low Income Countries: the Case Uganda* (London: London School of Economics, 6–7 July 2005).
Kainerugaba, Muhoozi, *Battles of the Ugandan Resistance: A Tradition of Manoeuvre* (Kampala: Fountain Publishers, 2010). ISBN 978-9970-25-032-5
Kalyegira, T., 'Insurgency in the Northern and Eastern Region in 1986' *monitor.co.ug*, (12 December 2012).
Kutesa, P., *Uganda's Revolution, 1979–1986: How I saw it* (Kampala: Fountain Publishers, 2006).
ISBN: 978-9970-02-564-0
Laffin J., *The World in Conflict; Contemporary Warfare Described and Analysed, War Annual* 7 (London: Brassey's, 1996).
ISBN: 1-85753-196-5
Lamwaka, C., 'The Peace Process in Northern Uganda, 1986–1990', *In Accord* Vol.11, (2002).
Museveni, Y. K., *Sowing the Mustard Seed* (London: MacMillan Education Ltd., 1997).
ISBN: 978-0333642344
Mutaizibwa, E., 'The Roots of War: How Alice Lakwena gave way to Joseph Kony', *observer.co.ug*, (11 August 2011).
Nyeko, B. & Lucima, O., 'Profiles of the Parties to the Conflict', *In Accord*, Vol. 11, (2002).
Oloya, O., *Child to Soldier: Stories from Joseph Kony's Lord's Resistance Army* (Toronto: University of Toronto Press, 2013).
ISBN 978-1442614178
Omara-Otunni, Amii, *Politics and the Military in Uganda*, 1890–1985 (London: MacMillan Press, 1987).
ISBN: 0-333-41980-4
Petermann, W., 'Die Flieger des Julius Nyerere', *Fliegerrevue Extra* agazine, Vol. 27 (September 2009).
Ruwehururu, B., *Cross to the Gun* (Kampala: Monitor, 2002).
ISBN 978-9970411658
Thompson, Sir R. (ed.), *War in Peace: An Analysis of Warfare since 1945* (London: Orbis Publishing, 1981).
ISBN: 0-85613-341-8
Turner, J., *Continent Ablaze: The Insurgency Wars in Africa, 1960 to the Present* (London: Arms and Armour Press, 1998).
ISBN: 1-85409-128-X
Wanambwa, R., 'Museveni: former UNLA Commander in Talks' *monitor.co.ug* (26 November 2014).
Weinstein, J. M., *Inside Rebellion: The Politics of Insurgent Violence* (Cambridge: Cambridge University Press, 2007).
ISBN : 978 0-521-67797-4
Wheeler, B. C., *An Illustrated Guide to Aircraft Markings* (London: Salamander Books Ltd, 1986).
ISBN: 0-86101-206-2
Willis D. (ed.), *Aerospace Encyclopaedia of World Air Forces* (London: Aerospace Publishing Ltd, 1999).
ISBN: 1-86184-045-4

Other publications:

Documentation of Teso Women's Experiences of Armed Conflict, 1987–2001 (ISIS-Women's International Cross Cultural Exchange, Kampala, 2002).
Let My People Go: The Forgotten Plight of the People in the Displaced Camps in Acholi (Acholi Religious Leaders Peace Initiative & Justice and Peace Commission, Gulu Archdiocese, 2001).
Occupation and Carnage; Recounting Atrocities Committed by the NRA's 35th Battalion in Namokora Sub-County in August 1986 (Justice & Reconciliation Project, Field Note XIX, March 2014; cited as JRP/FN XIX).
The Beasts at Burcoro; Recounting Atrocities by the NRA's 22nd Battalion in Burcoro Village in April 1991 (Justice & Reconciliation Project, Field Note XVII, July 2013; cited as JRP/FN XVII).
The Mukura Massacre of 1989 (Justice & Reconciliation Project, Field Note XII, March 2011; cited as JRP/FN XII).

ACKNOWLEDGEMENTS

Projects of this kind are always a matter of lots of networking and, indeed, teamwork. The authors relied greatly on co-operation with a number of individuals from around the world, who greatly helped collect relevant information and photographs. Some of them requested to remain anonymous and thus we can only express our gratitude to them in person. Among those we feel we can mention are: Fausto Biloslavo from Italy, who kindly provided his experience from trips to Uganda and many of the photographs he has taken there; Albert Grandolini from France, who shared many photographs from his extensive collection, or otherwise helped establish contacts to sources of information and photographs; and Dr Oliver Bangerter, from Switzerland, who provided plenty of knowledge about the NRA. Our special thanks are due to Pit Weinert from Germany, for sharing so much of his unique knowledge about the Tanzanian Air Force. We would also like to express our special thanks to Myriam Cornaz, for helping in preparing the manuscript. Last but not least, we would like to express our gratitude to our wives, for always patiently accompanying us, at all the times providing the support required to complete our research and 'put it to paper'.

ABOUT THE AUTHORS

Tom Cooper

Tom Cooper, from Austria, is a military-aviation journalist and historian. Following a career in a worldwide transportation business – in which, during his extensive travels in Europe and the Middle East, he established excellent contacts – he moved into writing. An earlier fascination with post-Second World War military aviation has narrowed to focus on smaller air forces and conflicts, about which he has collected extensive archives of material. Concentrating primarily on air warfare that has previously received scant attention, he specialises in investigative research on little-known African and Arab air forces, as well as the Iranian air force. Cooper has published 23 books – including the unique 'Arab MiGs' series, which examined the development and service history of major Arab air forces in conflicts with Israel – as well as over 250 articles on related topics, providing a window into a number of previously unexamined yet fascinating conflicts and relevant developments.

Adrien Fontanellaz

Adrien Fontanellaz, from Switzerland, is a military history researcher and author. He developed a passion for military history at an early age and has progressively narrowed his studies to modern-day conflicts. He is a member of the Scientific Committee of the Pully-based Centre d'histoire et de prospective militaires (Military History and Prospective Centre) and regularly contributes articles for the *Revue Militaire Suisse* and various French military history magazines. He is co-founder and a regular contributor to the the French military history website *L'autre côté de la colline*.